ACA Audit ar
Professional:
Preparation Kit

Copyright

Contents

4

Book Map

Exam Structure: Overview of the exam format, including types of questions and exam duration.

Syllabus Area: Summary of the main topics covered in the syllabus.

Skills Assessed: Description of the key skills evaluated in the exam, like analytical thinking.

Assimilating and Using Information: How to effectively gather and use information for audit purposes.

Structuring Problems and Solutions: Techniques for identifying problems and devising solutions in auditing.

Applying Judgement: Importance of using sound judgment in auditing decisions.

Concluding, Recommending and Communicating: Skills in finalizing audits, making recommendations, and communicating findings.

Technical Knowledge: Essential technical knowledge required for auditors.

The International Auditing and Assurance Standards Board: Information about the board and its role.

The Authority Attaching to Standards Issued by the IAASB: Understanding the authority and importance of these standards.

FRC Scope and Authority of Audit and Assurance Pronouncements: Scope and authority of Financial Reporting Council's pronouncements.

International Standards on Quality Management (ISQMs) (UK): Overview of quality management standards in the UK.

Quality Management for Firms: Guidelines for managing quality in audit firms.

Engagement Quality Reviews: Understanding the process and importance of engagement quality reviews.

International Standards on Auditing (UK): Overview of auditing standards applicable in the UK.

200 (Revised June 2016) (Updated May 2022) Overall Objectives: Objectives of independent auditors.

210 (Revised June 2016) Agreeing the Terms of Audit Engagements: Setting terms for audit engagements.

220 (Revised July 2021) Quality Management for an Audit: Quality management in audits.

230 (Revised June 2016) Audit Documentation: Importance of documentation in audits.

240 (Revised May 2021) The Auditor's Responsibilities Relating to Fraud: How auditors deal with potential fraud.

250 Section A (Revised November 2019) Consideration of Laws and Regulations: Understanding laws and regulations in auditing.

260 (Revised November 2019) Communication with Those Charged with Governance: Effective communication strategies with governance bodies.

265 Communicating Deficiencies in Internal Control: How to communicate internal control issues.

300 (Revised June 2016) Planning an Audit: Strategies for planning an effective audit.

315 (Revised July 2020) Identifying Risks of Material Misstatement: Identifying and assessing risks in financial statements.

320 (Revised June 2016) Materiality in Planning and Performing an Audit: Understanding the concept of materiality in audits.

330 (Revised July 2017) The Auditor's Responses to Assessed Risks: How auditors should respond to identified risks.

402 Audit Considerations for Entities Using a Service Organization: Special considerations for audits involving service organizations.

450 (Revised June 2016) Evaluation of Misstatements: Evaluating and addressing misstatements in audits.

500 Audit Evidence: Gathering and evaluating audit evidence.

501 Audit Evidence for Selected Items: Focusing on specific audit evidence.

505 External Confirmations: Using external sources to confirm audit information.

510 (Revised June 2016) Initial Audit Engagements: Managing initial audit engagements.

520 Analytical Procedures: Using analytical procedures in audits.

530 Audit Sampling: Techniques and importance of audit sampling.

540 (Revised December 2018) Auditing Accounting Estimates: Handling accounting estimates in audits.

550 Related Parties: Dealing with audits involving related parties.

560 Subsequent Events: Understanding and auditing subsequent events.

570 (Revised September 2019) Going Concern: Assessing the going concern assumption in audits.

580 Written Representations: Importance of written representations in audits.

600 (Revised September 2022) Audits of Group Financial Statements: Special considerations for group financial statement audits.

610 (Revised June 2013) Using the Work of Internal Auditors: Leveraging internal auditors' work.

620 (Revised November 2019) Using the Work of an Auditor's Expert: Utilizing experts in auditing.

700 (Revised November 2019) Forming an Opinion and Reporting: Formulating and reporting audit opinions.

701 (Revised November 2019) Communicating Key Audit Matters: How to communicate key audit matters.

705 (Revised June 2016) Modifications to the Opinion: Handling modifications to the audit opinion.

706 (Revised June 2016) Emphasis of Matter Paragraphs: Using emphasis of matter paragraphs in audit reports.

710 Comparative Information: Auditing comparative financial information.

720 (Revised November 2019) The Auditor's Responsibility for Other Information: Auditor's responsibilities beyond financial statements.

800 (Revised) Special Considerations for Special Purpose Frameworks: Audits for special purpose frameworks.

805 (Revised) Special Considerations for Single Financial Statements: Considerations for specific financial statement audits.

International Standards on Assurance Engagements (ISAEs) (UK): Overview of assurance engagement standards in the UK.

3000 (July 2020) Assurance Engagements Other Than Audits: Assurance engagements outside of standard audits.

International Standards on Review Engagements (ISREs): Overview of standards for reviewing financial statements.

2400 (Revised) Engagements to Review Historical Financial Statements: Conducting reviews of historical financial data.

International Standards on Review Engagements (UK): UK-specific standards for reviewing financial statements.

2410 (Revised May 2021) Review of Interim Financial Information: Reviewing interim financial information.

International Standards on Assurance Engagements (ISAEs): Global standards for assurance engagements.

3400 Examination of Prospective Financial Information: Auditing future financial projections.

3402 Assurance Reports on Controls at a Service Organisation: Reports on service organization controls.

3410 Assurance Engagements on Greenhouse Gas Statements: Auditing greenhouse gas emissions statements.

Other Guidance: Additional resources and guidelines for auditors.

Bulletin (August 2021): Illustrative Auditor's Reports: Examples of auditor's reports on UK private sector financial statements.

Azhar ul Haque Sario

Exam Structure

The ICAEW ACA UK Audit and Assurance exam is an important step for students aspiring to become professional auditors. Let's break down the structure and requirements of this exam in simple terms, making it easier for students to grasp and prepare effectively.

Duration and Format of the Exam
Length: The exam lasts for 2.5 hours. It's crucial to manage this time wisely during the exam.
Question Types: The exam comprises two types of questions:
Short-Form Questions: These are four or five in number. They are brief and typically focus on specific points or concepts. They require concise and direct answers.
Longer Questions: There are three of these, demanding more detailed responses. They test your understanding of concepts in depth.
Syllabus Areas and Weightings
The exam covers three main areas from the syllabus. Each area has a specific "weighting" or importance level in the exam:

Area 1: This might focus on fundamental principles of audit and assurance. Expect questions that test your basic understanding of these principles.
Area 2: Here, you might encounter scenarios that require the application of these principles in practical situations.
Area 3: This could involve higher-order thinking, like analyzing complex scenarios or evaluating different auditing strategies.
The "weightings" mentioned in the specification grid determine how much each area contributes to your

overall score. It's like a pie chart showing which parts of the syllabus are most important for the exam.

Preparation Tips
Understand the Syllabus: Familiarize yourself with the syllabus areas and their weightings. This helps in prioritizing your study.
Practice Time Management: Since the exam is time-bound, practice answering questions within a set time.
Study Material: Use recommended textbooks and study guides. They are tailored to cover all necessary topics.
Practice Papers: Attempt past exam papers. They give you a feel of the actual exam format and types of questions.
Conceptual Understanding: Focus on understanding concepts rather than rote memorization. This helps in answering longer, scenario-based questions.
Revision Plan: Create a study plan that allows you to revise each syllabus area adequately.
Real-Life Example
Consider a student, Alice. She allocated her study time based on the weightings of the syllabus areas. For the heavily weighted areas, she spent more time understanding and practicing different types of questions. She regularly attempted mock exams within the 2.5-hour timeframe, which improved her time management skills. By focusing on conceptual understanding, Alice was able to handle the longer questions in the exam more effectively.

Syllabus Area

Let's break down this syllabus area weighting for the ICAEW ACA UK Audit and Assurance module in a student-friendly manner. This syllabus structure is crucial for students preparing for this exam as it gives a clear picture of what topics are important and how much they contribute to the overall exam.

1. Legal and Other Professional Regulations, Ethics, Accepting and Managing Engagements and Current Issues (30%)
This section, making up 30% of your exam, is significant. It focuses on:

Legal and Other Professional Regulations: This covers the laws and guidelines you must follow as an auditor. You need to know what is legally allowed and what isn't in auditing.

Ethics: This is about doing the right thing, even when no one is watching. It includes understanding the moral principles that should guide an auditor's conduct.

Accepting and Managing Engagements: This is about knowing when to say yes to an auditing job and how to handle it. It includes understanding how to start, plan, and manage an audit assignment.

Current Issues: Stay updated! This includes any new changes or hot topics in the auditing world. For example, any recent changes in laws or auditing standards.

2. Planning and Performing Engagements (50%)
This is the heart of the exam, making up half of it. It's all about:

Planning Engagements: Before you start auditing, you need a plan. This involves understanding the company you're auditing, identifying areas where there might be problems, and deciding how you'll go about the audit.

Performing Engagements: This is the actual work of auditing. It means looking at the company's financial records, checking they're correct, and making sure the company is following all the rules.

3. Concluding and Reporting on Engagements (20%)
This final part, though smaller, is crucial. It involves:

Concluding Engagements: After all the auditing work, this is about making sense of what you've found. It's deciding if the company has been honest and fair in its financial reports.

Reporting on Engagements: This is about telling everyone what you've found. It includes preparing reports that explain your findings and conclusions in a clear and honest way.

Tips for Preparation
Focus on Understanding, Not Just Memorizing: Try to grasp the concepts behind the rules and procedures.

Stay Updated: Regularly check for updates in auditing standards and laws.

Practice Real-World Scenarios: Apply your knowledge to real-life situations; it helps in understanding the practical aspects of auditing.

Balance Your Study: Since planning and performing engagements is 50% of the exam, spend more time on it. But don't neglect the other sections.

Remember, each part of the syllabus is interconnected. Understanding ethics, for example, will help you in planning and performing engagements more ethically and professionally. Good luck with your studies!

Skills Assessed

Assimilating and Using Information

When preparing for the ICAEW ACA UK Audit and Assurance examination, it's crucial to have a deep understanding of the regulatory, professional, and ethical issues that are integral to accepting, carrying out, and managing assurance engagements. This knowledge not only helps in passing the exam but also in your professional conduct as an auditor.

Regulatory Issues
Compliance with Standards: Auditors must adhere to UK and international standards on auditing. This includes understanding updates and changes to the International Standards on Auditing (UK), as set by the Financial Reporting Council (FRC).

Legal Requirements: Auditors need to be aware of the legal context of their work, such as the Companies Act 2006, which sets out duties and responsibilities for auditors in the UK.

Reporting Obligations: Familiarity with the specific reporting requirements, including the need to report certain matters to the relevant authorities, is essential. For instance, under the UK's anti-money laundering regulations, auditors must report suspicious activities.

Professional Issues
Competence and Capability: Auditors must ensure they have the appropriate competence and capability to undertake an audit. This encompasses continuous professional development and staying updated with the

latest auditing techniques and sector-specific knowledge.

Objectivity and Independence: Maintaining objectivity and independence in all matters relating to the audit is paramount. This includes avoiding situations that might lead to conflicts of interest or the perception thereof.

Audit Documentation: Proper documentation of the audit work is crucial for quality control and peer review. This involves keeping detailed records of audit plans, work performed, evidence obtained, and conclusions drawn.

Ethical Issues
Confidentiality: Auditors are privy to sensitive information and must ensure that this information is kept confidential and not used for personal gain.

Integrity: Displaying honesty and straightforwardness in all professional and business relationships is vital. This includes not being associated with information that the auditor believes is materially false or misleading.

Real-Life Example
Consider the case of the Carillion collapse in 2018. The subsequent investigation highlighted several issues, such as the need for auditors to be more skeptical and challenge management assertions rigorously. This example underscores the importance of professional skepticism in audit engagements.

Studies and Resources
A study by the Association of Chartered Certified Accountants (ACCA) emphasized the evolving nature of audit and assurance services, pointing out the

increasing relevance of non-financial information in audits. This study illustrates the expanding scope of audit work and the need for auditors to adapt to these changes.

In the world of checking and making sure financial information is correct, especially in the UK with the ICAEW ACA, there's a super important set of steps called Quality Assurance (QA) processes. Think of these as the superhero toolkit for finding and stopping problems before they get out of hand. Let's dive into this toolkit and see how it works to keep things safe and sound.

Smart Planning: Imagine you're going on a treasure hunt. You wouldn't just wander off without a map, right? QA does something similar for audits. It makes a plan that's just right for each company, whether they're making apps or cars. There was this study by ICAEW that said good planning makes sure you don't miss the important stuff and use your team in the best way possible.

Teamwork and Double-Checks: It's like having a wise friend who checks your homework. In audits, the big bosses (senior auditors) keep an eye on the work, especially what the newbies do. This way, mistakes or big issues get caught early. There's this real-life story where this kind of teamwork found a huge mistake in a company's money report, stopping a big mess.

Playing Detective: Auditors have to be a bit like Sherlock Holmes, always questioning and not just taking things at face value. This helps them spot sneaky errors or even fraud. Remember the big Enron scandal?

It showed how important it is for auditors to be curious and not just believe everything they see.

Tech to the Rescue: Today's auditors use cool tech stuff like data-crunching tools and AI. This lets them look through tons of data to find things that don't add up. The ICAEW found that these high-tech tools are really good at catching weird stuff that might be hidden in the numbers.

Always Learning: Just like superheroes always learning new tricks, auditors keep updating their skills. When new rules come out, like those for how companies should record their sales, auditors get trained to understand what these changes mean for their work.

Talking it Out: Good auditors talk a lot with the companies they're checking. They explain what they're doing and listen to any worries the company might have. This clear chat helps avoid mix-ups and misunderstandings.

Staying True and Fair: Lastly, auditors stick to the rules of being honest and unbiased. They make sure they're not too chummy with the company they're auditing. It's like a referee in a game – they can't play favorites!

In the realm of audit and assurance, especially within the ICAEW ACA UK framework, the ability to identify relevant information through data analytics software is crucial. This skill isn't just about understanding the software; it's about interpreting the data in a way that enables actionable insights, guiding the audit process towards areas that need attention. Let's explore this in a simple yet comprehensive manner, weaving in real-life examples and technical insights.

Understanding the Data Landscape
Firstly, imagine you're an auditor with a massive dataset from a client. This data could include financial transactions, internal communications, or operational metrics. Your task is to sift through this sea of information to find what matters. Data analytics software is your submarine in this deep ocean. Tools like SQL, Python, or specific auditing software can help you navigate and organize this data.

Identifying Key Information
The key lies in knowing what to look for. In auditing, you're typically on the lookout for anomalies, trends, or deviations from the norm. For example, if you're analyzing a company's expenses, a sudden, unexplained spike in a particular category could be a red flag. The software can help you spot these outliers, but it's your understanding of the business and its context that tells you why they matter.

Real-Life Example
Consider the case of a retail company. By using data analytics, an auditor might notice that the inventory levels fluctuate oddly before and after stock takes. This could indicate issues like theft or mismanagement. In 2019, a study by the Association of Certified Fraud Examiners found that businesses lose an average of 5% of revenue to fraud each year. Data analytics plays a pivotal role in uncovering such discrepancies.

Suggesting Actions
Once you've identified these areas of concern, the next step is to suggest actions. This could involve deeper investigations into certain transactions, interviews with staff, or a review of internal controls. The aim is to not only identify the problem but also to help the business prevent it in the future.

Continuous Learning and Adaptation
The world of data analytics in audit and assurance is ever-evolving. Auditors must continuously update their skills and knowledge. For instance, the rise of machine learning and AI in data analytics offers new ways to detect fraud and inefficiencies.

Exam Preparation Tips
For ACA exam preparation, focus on understanding how data analytics tools work and their application in auditing scenarios. Practice case studies where you analyze datasets and make recommendations based on your findings. Remember, it's not just about using the software; it's about interpreting the data in a meaningful way.

In the field of audit and assurance, particularly within the ICAEW ACA framework in the UK, the ability to respond effectively to instructions from a line manager, partner, or client is a vital skill. This encompasses not only the technical aspects of auditing but also involves making informed judgments and considering ethical implications.

Understanding Instructions and Context
Clarification and Confirmation: Always ensure you fully understand the task. Ask questions if necessary and confirm your understanding. This avoids

misunderstandings and ensures that the work aligns with the expectations.

Contextual Understanding: Grasp the bigger picture. For instance, if a manager asks for a specific financial analysis, understand its role in the overall audit process. This helps in delivering more relevant and useful work.

Making Judgements
Analytical Thinking: Apply critical thinking to assess situations. For instance, if analyzing a company's financial statements, don't just look at numbers but understand what they mean in the company's context.

Professional Skepticism: Essential in auditing, this involves questioning and not taking information at face value. For example, if a client presents an unusually high expense, investigate and validate it.

Ethical Considerations
Confidentiality: Auditors often handle sensitive information. Maintaining confidentiality is not just ethical but often a legal requirement.

Integrity: Be honest and upright in your dealings. If you find discrepancies or areas of concern, report them accurately.

Real-Life Example
A study by the Association of Chartered Certified Accountants (ACCA) highlighted the importance of ethical judgement in audit and assurance. In a scenario where an auditor found financial discrepancies, those who weighed ethical considerations alongside technical aspects were better at resolving the issue effectively and maintaining integrity.

Technical Knowledge
Stay Updated: Audit and assurance is a constantly evolving field. Keep abreast of the latest IFRS updates, auditing standards, and technological advancements.

Understand the Tools: Be proficient with audit software and tools. This improves efficiency and accuracy.

Client Interaction
Effective Communication: Clearly articulate your findings and advice. Tailor your communication style to the audience - technical for fellow auditors, simpler for clients who may not have a financial background.

Responsiveness: Be prompt and proactive in your responses. This builds trust and credibility.

Structuring Problems and Solutions

Managing audit and other assurance engagements is a critical aspect of the ICAEW ACA qualification in the UK, particularly in the Audit and Assurance module. The key to mastering this area lies in understanding its complexities and applying practical knowledge skillfully. Let's delve into this subject by breaking it down into comprehensible sections, each illuminated with real-life examples and relevant studies.

1. Understanding the Audit Engagement Process
Audit engagements involve examining an organization's financial statements to ensure accuracy and compliance with accounting standards. The process typically starts with planning, where auditors assess risks and determine the nature, timing, and extent of the audit procedures. A study by the University of Oxford emphasized the importance of meticulous planning in reducing audit risks.

Real-life Example: In 2019, a major UK retail company faced financial discrepancies. An audit revealed that inadequate planning had led to oversight of significant financial misstatements.

2. Risk Assessment and Materiality
One of the primary tasks in an audit is to identify and assess risks of material misstatement. Materiality refers to the significance of an error or omission in financial statements that would mislead users. The auditor must set a materiality threshold, which helps in focusing on significant areas.

Real-life Example: A technology firm in London incorrectly valued its inventory, significantly impacting its financial position. The auditors, by setting an appropriate materiality level, were able to pinpoint and rectify this error.

3. Audit Evidence and Procedures
Gathering sufficient and appropriate audit evidence is essential. This can include inspection, observation, inquiry, confirmation, and computation. Auditors must use various procedures to corroborate the information presented in the financial statements.

Real-life Example: In an audit of a UK-based manufacturing company, auditors used physical inventory counts and third-party confirmations to verify asset valuations.

4. Using Technology in Audits
The integration of technology, like data analytics and AI, in audits is becoming increasingly important. These technologies can enhance the efficiency and effectiveness of audits.

Study Reference: A report by ACCA (Association of Chartered Certified Accountants) highlighted how data analytics is revolutionizing audit processes by enabling deeper insights into financial data.

5. Professional Skepticism and Judgment
Auditors must exercise professional skepticism and judgment throughout the audit process. This involves critically assessing audit evidence and being alert to conditions that may indicate possible misstatement.

Real-life Example: An auditor at a UK bank noticed discrepancies in loan provisioning figures. By exercising professional skepticism, they uncovered a significant understatement of loan loss provisions.

6. Communication and Reporting
Effective communication with the audited entity and within the audit team is crucial. The final step is the audit report, which provides the auditor's opinion on the financial statements.

Real-life Example: A UK charity's audit uncovered some minor compliance issues. The auditors effectively communicated these findings, enabling the charity to improve its financial practices.

7. Ethical Considerations
Ethical behavior, confidentiality, and independence are paramount in audit engagements. Auditors must avoid conflicts of interest and ensure their integrity is not compromised.

Study Reference: A 2020 survey by ICAEW highlighted the significance of ethics in maintaining public trust in financial reporting.

Reliance on controls is a pivotal concept in the realm of audit and assurance, particularly for those pursuing the ICAEW ACA qualification in the UK. Understanding this concept is not just about memorizing definitions; it's about grasping its practical applications and implications in the real world of auditing.

What is Reliance on Controls?
At its core, reliance on controls refers to the degree of confidence an auditor places in the client's internal control systems when planning and performing an

audit. Internal controls are processes and procedures implemented by a company to ensure the integrity of financial and accounting information, promote accountability, and prevent fraud.

Why is it Important?
In the context of an audit, if an auditor assesses that these controls are strong and reliable, they may decide to reduce the extent of substantive testing. This doesn't mean ignoring substantive procedures altogether but rather optimizing the audit process by focusing on areas where there's a higher risk of material misstatement.

Real-Life Application:
Consider a company with a robust system for processing and recording sales transactions. If an auditor, through a combination of tests of controls and other procedures, gains assurance that this system is effective in preventing and detecting errors, they might reduce the amount of detailed testing of sales transactions. However, this doesn't mean overlooking significant risks; it's about efficient resource allocation.

Studies and Technical Insights:
Research, such as that published in the Journal of Accounting and Economics, has often highlighted a direct correlation between the strength of internal controls and the accuracy of financial reporting. Auditors are trained to evaluate these controls critically, understanding that even the best systems can have weaknesses.

Risks and Challenges:
One major risk in relying on controls is overestimating their effectiveness. For example, if an auditor underestimates the risk of override of controls by

management, they might overlook significant misstatements. It's a balance of trust and skepticism.

Balancing Act in Auditing:
The auditor's reliance on controls is a balancing act – trusting the systems in place but also maintaining a level of professional skepticism. It requires a deep understanding of the business, its environment, and its internal control systems.

ACA Exam Preparation:
For ACA exam success, understanding reliance on controls is not just about knowing the theory; it's about applying it. Case studies and real-life scenarios provided in study materials are excellent for this. Pay attention to how changes in internal controls can alter the auditor's approach.

Embarking on the adventure of audit and assurance, especially under ICAEW ACA in the UK, let's explore the fascinating world of relying on internal audits and external experts. It's like assembling a puzzle, where each piece is crucial for the complete picture.

A Peek into the World of Internal Audits and External Wizards
Internal Audit Team: Imagine them as detectives within a company. They're the ones who scrutinize everything from how risks are handled to how well the company's plans are working. They're like the guardians of the company's inner workings.
External Experts: These folks are like the special guests on a TV show. They come with their superpowers in specific areas - think of a computer whiz or a legal eagle. Their knowledge is super valuable when the

regular audit team needs a bit of extra help in areas they're not experts in.

The Art of Balancing Trust and Caution

Checking the Credibility: It's like making a new friend. Before you rely on what they say, you want to know if they really know their stuff. Are they independent thinkers? Have they got a track record of being right?

Understanding Their Work: Imagine you're using a recipe from a famous chef. You'd want to know exactly what ingredients they used and how they cooked it. It's the same with using the work of these experts.

Stories from the Real World

Picture a factory where a machine expert helps the auditor figure out how much the machines are worth. It's like having a car expert tell you the value of a vintage car.

In a bank, the internal team checking how loans are given out is like having someone double-check that the rules of a game are being followed correctly.

Keeping a Sharp Eye

Even when you trust these experts, you still need to be like a wise owl - always watching and thinking, "Does this make sense?"

Writing It All Down

It's super important to jot down why and how much you trust these experts' work. It's like keeping a diary of your decisions so you can explain them later.

Fresh Insights and Learning

There are always new studies popping up, like those in the 'International Journal of Auditing'. These are like your regular updates on what's new and exciting in the world of auditing.

Handy Tips
Talk, Talk, Talk: Keep chatting with your internal teams and experts. Good communication is key.
Never Stop Learning: The world of auditing is always changing. Stay curious and keep learning.

When preparing for the ICAEW ACA examination in Audit and Assurance, particularly in the UK context, understanding the reliance on the work of another auditor is a critical aspect. This concept is not just a textbook theory; it's a practical reality in the complex world of auditing, especially when dealing with multinational corporations or companies with subsidiaries in different countries.

Definition and Importance
In simple terms, relying on the work of another auditor involves using the audit evidence and conclusions drawn by an auditor who has worked on a different but related part of the audit. Imagine a UK-based company with a subsidiary in Germany. The UK auditor might rely on the work done by the German auditor for the subsidiary's financials. This reliance is not just a matter of convenience but a necessity due to the geographical and jurisdictional complexities.

Governing Standards and Guidelines
The ICAEW, aligned with international standards like ISA (International Standards on Auditing), has specific guidelines on this matter. ISA 600 deals explicitly with this issue, providing a framework for the principal auditor (the one who audits the group financial statements) to evaluate and use the work of another auditor.

Real-Life Example

Consider the example of a multinational corporation, XYZ Ltd, headquartered in the UK. XYZ Ltd has multiple subsidiaries across Europe, each audited by local auditors. The group auditor, based in the UK, must consolidate these individual audits into a single group audit. Here, the principle of relying on another auditor's work becomes crucial. The UK auditor must assess the competence, capabilities, and objectivity of the local auditors, ensuring that their work aligns with the required audit standards and can be reliably used for the group audit.

Evaluating the Other Auditor's Work

The evaluation involves several key steps:

Assessment of Professional Competence: Ensuring that the other auditor has the necessary skills, experience, and knowledge.

Understanding the Other Auditor's Work: This includes reviewing their audit plan, methods, and conclusions.

Compliance with Standards: Confirming that the other auditor's work complies with the relevant auditing standards.

Challenges and Risks

Relying on another's work is not without challenges. The principal auditor must be wary of:

Differences in Audit Standards: Auditing standards might vary between countries.

Quality of Work: The quality of the other auditor's work directly impacts the group audit.

Communication Barriers: Effective communication is key, and language or cultural differences can pose challenges.

Case Studies and Research
Several case studies and research papers have explored the dynamics and implications of this reliance. For instance, a study by the Auditing Practices Board (UK) highlighted the importance of clear communication and detailed documentation when relying on the work of another auditor.

In the context of the ICAEW ACA UK Audit and Assurance, understanding the extent of tests of control and substantive procedures, including analytical procedures, is crucial for exam preparation. Let's delve into these concepts, incorporating real-life examples and relevant studies, to enhance your understanding in a comprehensive yet simple manner.

1. Tests of Control
Tests of control are designed to assess the effectiveness of a company's internal controls. They involve procedures to test the functioning of these controls over a period.

Extent of Testing: The extent here refers to the volume and frequency of tests. For example, if a company has a strong history of effective internal controls, the auditor may decide to perform fewer tests of control. Conversely, if there are indications of potential control weaknesses, more extensive testing is required.

Real-Life Example: Consider a retail company with an electronic sales system. An auditor might test the system's access controls, ensuring that only authorized personnel can process refunds, to mitigate the risk of fraudulent transactions.

2. Substantive Procedures
Substantive procedures are direct tests of financial transactions and balances to detect material misstatements. They are of two types: tests of detail and substantive analytical procedures.

Tests of Detail: These involve verifying the accuracy of individual transactions and balances. For instance, confirming outstanding receivables by directly contacting customers.

Substantive Analytical Procedures: This involves assessing financial information through analysis and comparison. For example, comparing current year sales figures with the previous year to identify significant variances that could indicate errors or fraud.

Extent of Testing: The extent depends on the risk of material misstatement. High-risk areas require more extensive substantive testing.

3. Analytical Procedures

Extent of Use: They are used at all stages of the audit: as a risk assessment tool, as a substantive procedure, and in the final review stage.

Example: An auditor might compare the company's payroll costs with the number of employees to spot inconsistencies that could indicate payroll fraud or errors.

Studies and Technical Knowledge
A study by the Auditing Practices Board found that the extent of both tests of control and substantive procedures varies significantly based on the auditor's perception of risk and materiality. The study highlighted the importance of professional judgment in determining the scope and extent of audit procedures.

Real-Life Application
In practice, an auditor working on a company with high turnover might place greater emphasis on substantive tests of revenue recognition, while in a smaller company, a detailed test of control over cash receipts could be more relevant.

Analytical procedures, including data analytic routines, play a crucial role in the audit and assurance processes, particularly in the ICAEW ACA context in the UK. These methods are not just tools for auditors; they are essential components that drive the effectiveness and efficiency of an audit. Let's dive deep into how these procedures help in identifying the risk of misstatement.

1. Understanding and Planning:
At the initial stages of an audit, analytical procedures assist in understanding the client's business and industry. By analyzing financial data trends and ratios, auditors gain insights into business operations, which is pivotal for planning the audit strategy. For example, a sudden increase in inventory turnover might prompt further investigation into inventory management practices.

2. Risk Assessment:
One of the primary uses of analytical procedures is in assessing the risk of material misstatement. By comparing current financial data with prior periods, budgets, and industry benchmarks, auditors can identify unusual fluctuations or trends. For instance, if an organization's profit margin deviates significantly from industry norms, it might indicate risks related to revenue recognition or cost control.

3. Directing Audit Efforts:
Analytical procedures help in directing audit efforts towards areas of higher risk. By identifying key risk indicators, auditors can allocate more resources and apply more rigorous audit procedures to those areas. A real-life example could be a company showing a consistent decrease in debt-to-equity ratio, which might lead auditors to focus more on debt covenants and long-term liabilities.

4. Substantive Analytical Procedures:
During the substantive testing phase, analytical procedures are used to validate financial statement assertions. For example, comparing the actual revenue with forecasted figures can provide evidence about the accuracy and completeness of revenue recognition.

5. Final Review:
In the final stages of the audit, analytical procedures provide an overall conclusion on the financial statements. Any significant deviations from expected trends or ratios are investigated to ensure that the financial statements as a whole are free from material misstatement.

6. Leveraging Data Analytics:
With advancements in technology, data analytics have become an integral part of analytical procedures. Tools like AI and machine learning can process large volumes of data to identify patterns and anomalies that would be impossible for a human auditor to detect manually. For example, data analytics can be used to identify unusual transactions in large datasets, such as duplicate payments or unusual journal entries.

Studies and Real-Life Application:
Studies have shown that the use of data analytics in audit significantly enhances the ability to detect fraud and errors. A study by the American Accounting Association found that data analytic techniques, such as Benford's Law analysis, were effective in identifying fictitious transactions in financial statements.

When preparing for the ICAEW ACA qualification, particularly the Audit and Assurance module, understanding the dynamics of assurance visits is crucial. These visits are a fundamental aspect of auditing, providing the necessary evidence and insights to form an audit opinion. Let's delve into the number, timing, staffing, and location of assurance visits, incorporating real-life examples and technical knowledge to enhance your understanding.

1. Number of Assurance Visits:
The number of assurance visits varies based on the complexity and size of the entity being audited. For example, a multinational corporation may require multiple visits due to its vast operations, while a small local business might need only one or two. The key is to ensure sufficient coverage to form a reliable audit opinion. For instance, if a company has multiple

branches or significant inventory holdings, each requiring individual attention, the number of visits will increase.

2. Timing of Visits:
Timing is critical in auditing. Assurance visits are often scheduled at different stages of the audit. Initial visits might occur at the planning stage to understand the business and its environment. Subsequent visits may focus on testing controls and substantive procedures. For instance, visiting a retail business during peak sales periods can provide valuable insights into inventory and cash handling processes. Also, year-end visits are common to observe inventory counts and gather evidence on year-end balances.

3. Staffing of Visits:
Staffing for assurance visits depends on the audit's scope and complexity. A team typically includes a mix of junior auditors, senior auditors, and a manager or partner. Each member plays a specific role, from detailed testing to overseeing the audit process. For example, junior auditors might perform tests on transactions, while senior auditors review their work and focus on more complex areas of the audit. The presence of a manager or partner ensures overall quality and compliance with auditing standards.

4. Location of Visits:
The location is determined by where the significant activities of the audited entity occur. This could be the head office, manufacturing plants, or branch offices. For instance, auditing a manufacturing company might require visits to factories to observe production processes and inventory controls. In some cases,

auditors might also need to visit third-party warehouses where the audited entity's inventory is stored.

Real-life example: Consider the audit of a large supermarket chain. The number of visits would be determined by the number of significant locations – perhaps key stores and distribution centers. Timing would be aligned with critical business cycles, like quarterly inventory counts or year-end financial closing. The staffing would involve a mix of skills, with junior auditors performing basic inventory counts and senior staff focusing on complex areas like revenue recognition. Locations would include stores, warehouses, and the head office.

Applying Judgement

Embarking on the journey to ace the ICAEW ACA UK Audit and Assurance exam, it's like stepping into a world where you're a detective, uncovering risks and mysteries within a company's financial landscape.

Unraveling the Mystery of Business and Audit Risks Imagine you're a detective in a vast corporate city. Your first task? Spotting the sneaky culprits - business risks. These are tricky elements that can throw a company off its success path. Picture a trendy clothing store suddenly losing its charm because the fashion tide turned. That's a business risk right there!

Next up, audit risks. These are like hidden traps in financial statements that might trick you into believing everything's fine when it's not. It's a three-headed monster comprising:

Inherent Risk: This one's sneaky by nature, like a high-tech gadget that's tough to understand.
Control Risk: Imagine a guard dog that's supposed to protect a house but sleeps on the job.
Detection Risk: This is when you, the detective, might miss a crucial clue.
The Ripple Effect on Financial Statements
Now, these risks can stir up a storm in the financial statements. Think of a boat (the company) that looks fine but has a leak (the risk) – it could sink if not fixed. If a business doesn't shout out about its troubles in the financial report, investors might think it's smooth sailing when it's actually heading towards a storm.

Crafting Your Detective Toolkit

As a financial detective, your toolkit to outsmart these risks includes:

Analytical Glasses: Put these on to see beyond the numbers. A sudden drop in sales? Could be a sign something's off.

Control Testing Magnifier: Check if the company's safety nets, like alarm systems (internal controls), actually work.

Substantive Detective Kit: This is your deep-dive gear. Check every nook and cranny – are those assets real, or just smoke and mirrors?

A Tale from the Trenches

Let's take a real-life detour. Imagine a tech company, "FutureTech," diving into new waters (markets). Business risks? The new crowd might not cheer for them. Audit risks? Keep an eye on how they record their sales. You'd have to dig deeper, checking contracts and confirming sales to ensure no fishy business is going on.

In the field of audit and assurance, particularly within the ICAEW ACA framework in the UK, understanding the quality of data and evidence is paramount. Here, we'll explore two crucial aspects: differentiating between internally generated and third-party data, and recognizing bias in evidence, especially when it's linked to elements like profit-based bonuses for management.

1. Internally Generated vs. Third-Party Data
Internally Generated Data:

Origin: Produced within the organization.

Characteristics: Often aligned with internal procedures and goals.
Risk: Higher susceptibility to management bias. Management may unintentionally or intentionally influence the data to present the organization more favorably.
Third-Party Data:

Origin: Created by external entities (e.g., suppliers, independent market reports).
Characteristics: Generally considered more objective.
Risk: Lower risk of management bias but requires validation for relevance and accuracy.
Real-World Example: Consider a company's internal financial reports versus an independent audit report by an accounting firm. The former, while insightful, might be influenced by the desire to show improved performance. The latter, being external, is less likely to be swayed by such internal motivations.

2. Bias in Evidence and Its Impact
Bias in evidence can significantly affect the quality and reliability of the data. This is especially true in scenarios where financial outcomes, like bonuses, are tied to performance metrics.

Examples of Bias:

Performance-Linked Bonuses: If bonuses are tied to profits, there might be a tendency to overstate earnings or understate expenses.

Subjective Judgments: Personal biases in estimating allowances for bad debts or valuing inventory can skew financial statements.
Mitigating Bias:

Auditors must be aware of these biases and apply professional skepticism.
Analyzing trends and comparing with industry benchmarks can help identify anomalies.
External corroboration, like third-party valuations, can provide a more objective view.
Case Study Reference: A study by the Journal of Accountancy found that companies with incentive-based compensation plans were more likely to use aggressive earnings management techniques. This underscores the need for auditors to be vigilant about biases that can creep into financial statements.

Getting ready for the ICAEW ACA UK Audit and Assurance exam? It's a journey into how the world outside affects the numbers inside a company's financial statements. Let's break this down into bite-sized, simple insights, mixing things up with different kinds of sentences and sprinkling in some real-world examples.

Economic Factors: Think of a company as a boat and the economy as the sea. When the sea is rough (like high inflation or low economic growth), the boat rocks (meaning the company's money matters get shaky). In 2008, big banks felt this when the financial storm hit, and their numbers turned red with losses.

Political Factors: Now imagine a game where the rules keep changing. That's what politics can do to a company's finances. A new tax law can change how much money a company keeps. Take Brexit – it was like a game-changer for many businesses in the UK and Europe, juggling their trade costs, rules, and even the value of their money.

Sustainability-Related Factors: It's like looking after your garden so it stays green and healthy. Companies today need to think about being good to the environment and society. This might cost them a bit more now (like buying better tools for the garden), but it can help them grow in the long run. A study from Harvard in 2011 showed that companies who really care about these things often do better than those who don't.

Climate-Related Factors: Imagine if your garden was suddenly hit by extreme weather. That's what climate change can do to businesses. Big events, like the 2019 Australian bushfires, can damage a lot of things and cost a lot of money, especially for insurance companies. Plus, there are new rules coming up to help stop climate change, and companies need to show how they're getting ready for this in their numbers.

When evaluating the effect of uncertain future events during the examination of a company's financial forecasts, auditors need to approach the task with a blend of analytical skills, professional skepticism, and a thorough understanding of the business and its environment. This is crucial for the ICAEW ACA qualification in the UK, particularly in the Audit and Assurance paper.

Understanding Business Context: First, auditors should immerse themselves in understanding the business context. This means gaining insights into the industry, market trends, the company's operational model, and its strategic objectives. For example, a tech company might be heavily influenced by rapid technological changes, whereas a manufacturing firm might be more impacted by supply chain disruptions.

Assessing Risk Factors: Auditors should identify and evaluate risk factors that can influence future events. These include external factors like economic conditions, regulatory changes, and internal factors such as management capability and operational efficiency. A study by the Audit Analytics (2019) showed that businesses with weak internal controls were more likely to revise their financial forecasts.

Scenario Analysis: Performing scenario analysis is a powerful tool. This involves creating various plausible future scenarios (e.g., optimistic, pessimistic, most likely) and assessing how these scenarios would impact the financial forecasts. For instance, how would a significant rise in raw material costs affect the company's profitability?

Review Historical Accuracy: Analyzing the accuracy of past forecasts can offer valuable insights. If a company has historically been overly optimistic in its forecasting, this might indicate a need for more conservative estimates.

Analyzing Assumptions: Every financial forecast is based on certain assumptions. It's vital to critically evaluate these assumptions for their reasonableness and the likelihood of occurrence. For example, if a forecast assumes a steady growth rate, is this aligned with industry trends and the company's historical performance?

Professional Skepticism: Maintaining professional skepticism is key. Auditors should question the evidence and not take information at face value. They should cross-verify data from multiple sources to ensure its reliability.

Use of Technology: Modern auditing increasingly involves data analytics and forecasting tools. These technologies can help in analyzing large datasets and trends, providing a more robust basis for evaluating forecasts.

Communication with Management: Engaging in open discussions with the company's management and challenging their assumptions and projections is essential. This helps in understanding the rationale behind the forecasts and identifying any biases.

Documentation: Finally, it's important to document the process, findings, and rationale for any conclusions drawn. This documentation should be comprehensive, clear, and structured, enabling any reviewer to understand the auditor's reasoning.

When preparing for the ICAEW ACA UK Audit and Assurance examination, understanding how to assess materiality in financial statements or other financial information is crucial. Materiality is a key concept in auditing and assurance, guiding auditors in making informed judgments about the significance of misstatements and unadjusted errors in financial reports.

Materiality assessment involves determining the magnitude of an omission or misstatement of accounting information that, in the light of surrounding circumstances, makes it probable that the judgment of a reasonable person. This concept is rooted in the notion that not all errors or omissions are equally significant in the context of an entity's financial statements.

Real-Life Example:
Imagine a large corporation that forgot to record a minor transaction worth £1,000 in a year where they reported £10 million in revenue. While the error is technically a mistake, its impact on the overall financial statements is minimal, likely not altering a stakeholder's opinion of the company's financial health.

Technical Knowledge:
According to ISA 320 (International Standards on Auditing), the auditor should consider materiality both when planning and performing the audit. Materiality is not a fixed threshold but a subjective measure that depends on the size and specific circumstances of the entity being audited.

Assessing Materiality:

Quantitative Factors: Typically, auditors consider a percentage of a financial benchmark, like total revenue, net income, or assets. For example, an error greater than 5% of net income might be considered material.
Qualitative Factors: Some errors, while small in monetary terms, may be qualitatively material. For example, a small misstatement that affects a key performance indicator or breaches a loan covenant is significant.
Modifying the Auditor's Opinion:
If after assessing materiality, the auditor concludes that an unadjusted error is material to the financial

statements, they must decide whether to modify their opinion in the auditor's report. There are different types of modified opinions:

Qualified Opinion: If the misstatement is material but not pervasive.
Adverse Opinion: If the misstatement is both material and pervasive.
Disclaimer of Opinion: When the auditor is unable to obtain sufficient appropriate audit evidence.
Non-Audit Assurance Reports:
In non-audit assurance engagements, similar principles apply. If a material misstatement is identified, the auditor needs to modify their conclusion. This might involve explaining the reasons for the modification and discussing the implications of the misstatement on the report.

Case Studies:
Studies like the one by PCAOB (Public Company Accounting Oversight Board) in the USA often review audit deficiencies and highlight the importance of proper materiality assessment. For example, PCAOB inspections have found instances where auditors failed to appropriately assess materiality, leading to significant audit failures.

When preparing for the ICAEW ACA UK Audit and Assurance exam, it's essential to understand the complexities surrounding the independence risks in audit engagements and the procedures for mitigating these risks, as well as the necessary steps to take upon discovering fraud or money laundering.

1. Judging Potential Independence Risks

Independence risks in audit or assurance engagements can arise from various scenarios. These risks are primarily concerned with situations where an auditor's ability to make impartial audit judgments is, or could be, compromised. A real-life example could be an auditor auditing a company where they have a financial interest.

Types of Independence Risks

Self-interest risk: This occurs when an auditor has a financial or other interest in the client. For example, owning shares in the client's business.

Self-review risk: This happens when the auditor reviews work that they or their firm have previously performed. For instance, auditing financial statements that they initially helped prepare.

Advocacy risk: When an auditor promotes a client's position or opinion to the point where it compromises their objectivity. This could happen if an auditor is advocating for a client in litigation or dispute.

Familiarity risk: Arising when an auditor becomes too sympathetic to the client's interests due to a close relationship. This could be a situation where the auditor has a relative working in a senior position at the client company.

Intimidation risk: This occurs when the auditor is deterred from acting objectively due to threats, actual or perceived, from the client.

Procedures to Mitigate Risks

To mitigate these risks, the following procedures are commonly implemented:

Establishing Safeguards: This includes creating policies that prevent or limit the extent of threats. For example, rotating audit team members regularly.

Professional Distance: Maintaining an appropriate professional relationship with the client, avoiding close personal relationships.

Transparency and Disclosure: Disclosing any potential conflicts of interest to relevant stakeholders.

2. Steps Upon Discovery of Fraud/Money Laundering

Discovering fraud or money laundering during an audit requires immediate and precise action. The auditor's steps should be:

Documenting the Finding: Record all details of the suspected fraud or money laundering.

Assessing the Impact: Determine how the finding affects the financial statements and the audit opinion.

Reporting to Management and Governance: Informing the appropriate level of management and, if necessary, those charged with governance.

Legal Obligations: Depending on the jurisdiction, there may be a legal obligation to report the findings to external authorities, like the National Crime Agency in the UK.

Re-evaluating Client Relationship: Consider whether it's appropriate to continue the audit engagement, given the discovery.

Real-Life Example

A notable case study is the Enron scandal, where auditors failed to report significant fraud. This case highlights the importance of auditors maintaining independence and taking decisive action when fraud is suspected.

Presenting a structured argument to a client, particularly in contexts where management questions the extent of audit work performed, is a crucial skill for professionals in the field of Audit and Assurance, especially under the guidelines of the ICAEW (Institute of Chartered Accountants in England and Wales) ACA (Associate Chartered Accountant) qualification in the UK.

1. Understanding the Importance of Communication:
In audit and assurance, communication isn't just about conveying information; it's about persuading and building trust. When management questions your audit work, it reflects a gap in understanding or trust. Your argument needs to bridge this gap. This involves not only technical audit knowledge but also an understanding of human psychology and organizational behavior.

2. Building Your Argument:
A structured argument is built upon clear, logical steps:

State Your Objective: Begin by clearly stating the objective of your audit work. For instance, "The aim of our audit is to provide reasonable assurance that the financial statements are free from material misstatement."
Provide Context: Explain the regulatory and professional standards that guide your work (e.g., ICAEW standards, International Standards on Auditing).
Detail the Work Performed: Clearly outline the procedures and tests you conducted. This might include sampling methods, the types of transactions reviewed, and any key controls tested.
Present Findings and Conclusions: Share the outcomes of your audit work. Where discrepancies or areas of concern were identified, explain them concisely.
Link Back to the Objective: Conclude by tying your findings back to the audit's objective, affirming the value and necessity of the work performed.

3. Anticipating and Addressing Concerns:
Understand the client's perspective. Why are they questioning the audit? Is it due to cost, time, or a lack of understanding of audit processes? Address these concerns directly in your argument. For instance, if cost is a concern, explain the potential financial and reputational risks of undetected material misstatements.

4. Real-Life Example:
Consider the case study of a UK-based company, XYZ Ltd., which questioned the extent of inventory checks performed during their audit. The auditors effectively presented their argument by:

Explaining the risk of material misstatement in inventory due to its size and complexity.
Detailing the statistical sampling method used and why it was appropriate.
Highlighting discrepancies found and how they could impact the financial statements.
Emphasizing the compliance with ICAEW and ISA standards, thus ensuring credibility and thoroughness.
5. The Human Element:
Remember, an argument isn't just about facts; it's also about perception. Be empathetic, patient, and open to dialogue. Building rapport with the client can often be as important as the technical content of your argument.

6. Continuous Learning and Adaptation:
Stay informed about the latest developments in audit standards and practices. Regularly attending ICAEW seminars or workshops, and reading relevant case studies or journals, can provide fresh insights and examples that can be used in discussions with clients.

Concluding, Recommending and Communicating

Navigating the world of assurance engagements, especially in the context of the ICAEW ACA UK Audit and Assurance exam, is like exploring a complex maze filled with specific rules and ethical paths to follow. Let's simplify this journey and look at it through a more creative lens.

1. The Rulebook (Regulatory Issues):

Following the Map: Imagine auditors as explorers who need a map. In their world, this map is the International Standards on Auditing (UK and Ireland). It shows them how to plan their journey, what paths to take, and how to tell others about their adventure.
Legal Compass: Just like a compass guides you north, laws like the Companies Act guide auditors to do the right thing legally.
Flying Solo (Auditor Independence): Think of auditors as lone wolves, who must not get too cozy with the entity they're auditing. It's all about staying unbiased and objective.
2. Professionalism: The Explorer's Code (Professional Issues):

Skill and Care: Auditors should be like skilled climbers, always prepared and careful on their ascent.
Secret Keepers: They know all sorts of secrets about the businesses they audit. But just like a trusted friend, they keep these secrets to themselves.
Learning Never Ends (CPD): The world of auditing constantly changes. So, auditors always keep learning, just like a doctor or a scientist would.

3. Ethics: The Moral Compass (Ethical Issues):

Truth and Fairness: Auditors should always be honest and fair, like a good referee in a game.
No Bias: They need to stay neutral, not favoring one side, much like a judge in a court.
Honor the Badge: They should behave in a way that makes everyone respect auditors.
Real-world Stories:

The Carillion Story (2018): Think of this like a blockbuster movie where the heroes (auditors) missed vital clues, leading to a big company's fall. This tale reminds everyone in auditing to be more vigilant.
Patisserie Valerie's Plot Twist (2019): A shocking story where everyone thought the company was doing great, but suddenly, it wasn't. It was a wake-up call for auditors to dig deeper.
Lessons from Research:

A study by the FRC (kind of like the wise council of the auditing world) said that the best audits happen when auditors stick to strong ethical values. It's like saying, the better the character of the auditor, the better the audit.

Concluding and reporting on assurance engagements, particularly in the context of determining whether to modify a report with or without a modified opinion or conclusion, is a crucial aspect of the audit and assurance process as outlined by the Institute of Chartered Accountants in England and Wales (ICAEW) ACA qualification. Let's delve into this topic in a detailed yet simple manner, tailored to help you prepare effectively for your examination.

Understanding the Basics of Assurance Engagements

An assurance engagement involves an independent auditor assessing various aspects of a company's operations, financials, or compliance. The primary goal is to provide stakeholders, like shareholders or regulators, with an assurance that the subject matter is free from material misstatement.

The Decision to Modify a Report
The decision to modify an audit report arises when the auditor encounters situations that prevent them from expressing an unmodified opinion. These situations can include:

Limitations on the Scope of the Audit: When the auditor cannot obtain sufficient appropriate audit evidence.
Material Misstatements: These could be due to error or fraud and are significant enough to affect the user's understanding of the report.
Going Concern Issues: Doubts about the entity's ability to continue as a going concern.
Types of Modified Opinions/Conclusions
Qualified Opinion: Suggests that except for certain areas, the financial statements give a true and fair view.
Adverse Opinion: Indicates that the misstatements are so material and pervasive that the financial statements do not present a true and fair view.
Disclaimer of Opinion: Issued when the auditor cannot obtain sufficient, appropriate evidence and the possible effects could be material and pervasive.
Real-Life Example
Consider a company, XYZ Ltd, undergoing an audit. The auditor finds that a significant portion of XYZ's inventory is not verifiable due to its location in a

conflict zone. This limitation could lead to a qualified opinion if the rest of the financial statements are found to be accurate.

Technical Aspects and Rare Knowledge
Materiality Judgment: Auditors must exercise professional judgment to determine the materiality of misstatements.
Ethical Considerations: Auditors must adhere to ethical principles, including objectivity and confidentiality.
ISA (International Standards on Auditing): Familiarity with ISA standards is crucial, as they guide the audit process, including report modifications.
Recent Studies and Developments
Studies have shown that the quality of the audit report significantly influences investor confidence. A paper by the Journal of Accountancy highlighted the importance of transparent and detailed audit reports in enhancing the credibility of financial information.

Identifying deficiencies in financial information systems is a crucial aspect of the audit and assurance process, especially for those pursuing the ICAEW ACA qualification in the UK. A robust understanding of these deficiencies, their potential consequences, and appropriate recommendations for improvement is essential for any aspiring auditor.
Identifying Deficiencies
Inaccurate Data Entry: One common deficiency is human error in data entry. This can lead to incorrect financial statements. For example, if an employee mistakenly enters £10,000 instead of £100,000, it significantly alters the financial outlook of the company.

Outdated Systems: Many companies still use outdated software, which can be prone to errors and inefficiencies. A 2019 study by Forrester revealed that outdated financial systems could lead to a 30% increase in operational costs.

Lack of Integration: Systems that do not integrate well with each other can lead to data silos, where information is not shared effectively across the organization. This can result in a lack of coherence in financial reporting.

Inadequate Security Measures: With the rise in cyber threats, a lack of robust security measures in financial information systems can lead to data breaches, affecting both the company's finances and reputation.

Insufficient Regulatory Compliance: Systems that are not updated to comply with the latest financial regulations can lead to legal issues and hefty fines.

Potential Consequences
Financial Losses: Errors in financial data can lead to significant financial losses. For instance, incorrect budget allocations based on faulty data can lead to overspending.

Reputational Damage: Data breaches or regulatory non-compliance can tarnish a company's reputation, leading to loss of customer trust.

Operational Disruption: Inefficient systems can slow down processes, affecting the company's ability to operate effectively.

Legal Repercussions: Non-compliance with financial regulations can result in legal actions against the company.

Recommendations for Improvement
Implementing Robust Software Solutions: Upgrading to more sophisticated, integrated software can enhance accuracy and efficiency. Software like SAP or Oracle Financials are popular choices.

Regular Training and Audits: Ensuring that staff are well-trained in using the systems and conducting regular audits can help identify and rectify errors promptly.

Enhancing Security Protocols: Investing in cybersecurity measures to protect financial data is crucial in today's digital age.

Staying Updated with Regulations: Regularly updating systems to comply with the latest financial regulations is key to avoiding legal issues.

Developing a Culture of Accuracy: Fostering a workplace culture that values accuracy and attention to detail can significantly reduce human errors.

Real-Life Example
Consider the case of a small business that faced significant financial discrepancies due to outdated accounting software. The business switched to an integrated cloud-based system, which not only corrected the inaccuracies but also streamlined their financial processes, leading to a 20% reduction in operational costs over the next year.

Technical Knowledge

The International Auditing and Assurance Standards Board

The International Auditing and Assurance Standards Board (IAASB) plays a crucial role in shaping the audit and assurance profession globally, especially impacting the ICAEW ACA Audit and Assurance module in the UK. Understanding the IAASB standards is not just about memorizing rules; it's about grasping the spirit and intent behind them. Let's delve into this topic with a blend of simplicity, creativity, and depth, perfect for your examination preparation.

Understanding IAASB Standards: A Simple Guide
Nature of IAASB Standards: These are sets of principles that guide auditors on various aspects of auditing and assurance services. They ensure consistency, reliability, and quality in audits across different countries and contexts.

Key Standards: The IAASB issues several standards, but some of the most critical ones include:

ISA (International Standards on Auditing): These are guidelines for financial statement audits. They cover everything from planning an audit to evaluating its findings.
ISRE (International Standards on Review Engagements): These apply to the review of financial statements, a task less comprehensive than an audit but still crucial.

ISAE (International Standards on Assurance Engagements): This category includes standards for assurance engagements other than audits or reviews. Real-Life Application: Imagine you're auditing a multinational company. The ISA standards guide you through the process, ensuring that your audit in the UK is consistent with an audit of the same company in another country. This uniformity is critical for stakeholders who rely on these financial statements globally.

Recent Changes and Developments: The IAASB constantly updates its standards to reflect changes in the business environment. For instance, recent updates have focused on areas like technology's impact on auditing and the growing importance of non-financial information in assurance engagements.

Impact on ICAEW ACA Exam: In your exam, expect scenarios where you'll apply these standards to practical situations. This might include identifying which standard applies to a specific scenario or explaining how to conduct an audit in compliance with these standards.

Study Tips:

Understand, Don't Just Memorize: Grasp the purpose behind each standard. Why was it introduced? What problem does it solve?
Practice with Scenarios: Use real-world examples or case studies to see how these standards are applied in practice.
Stay Updated: Regularly check the IAASB website for updates or amendments to the standards.

The Authority Attaching to Standards Issued by the International Auditing and Assurance Standards Board

When preparing for the ICAEW ACA UK Audit and Assurance examination, understanding the authority that attaches to the standards issued by the International Auditing and Assurance Standards Board (IAASB) is crucial. The IAASB, a globally recognized independent standard-setting body, plays a pivotal role in shaping auditing practices and assurance engagements worldwide. Let's delve into the specifics of their standards' authority and implications, especially for UK auditing.

Global Recognition and Adoption: The standards set by the IAASB, such as International Standards on Auditing (ISAs), are globally recognized. They provide a benchmark for auditing quality and consistency across different countries. For UK auditors, this global recognition implies that adhering to these standards is not just a local requirement but part of a broader, internationally accepted best practice. This global framework fosters trust and confidence in financial reports across borders.

Compliance with Regulatory Frameworks: In the UK, the Financial Reporting Council (FRC) adopts and adapts these international standards to fit the UK context, forming the basis of UK auditing standards. Compliance with these standards is not optional; it's a regulatory requirement. Auditors must adhere to these standards to ensure their audit opinions are valid, credible, and legally defensible.

Quality Assurance and Professional Reputation: The standards serve as a cornerstone for quality assurance in auditing. They provide detailed guidance on audit planning, execution, and reporting. By following these standards, auditors can assure clients and stakeholders of the reliability and thoroughness of their audit processes. A reputation for quality and adherence to high standards is essential for building trust and maintaining a professional standing in the field.

Legal and Ethical Implications: IAASB standards also encompass ethical principles. Non-compliance can have legal implications, ranging from professional sanctions to legal action. In the UK, auditors are expected to not only perform their duties competently but also ethically, aligning with the principles outlined in these standards.

Continuous Professional Development: The dynamic nature of business and regulation means that IAASB standards are regularly updated. This demands continuous learning and adaptation from UK auditors. Staying updated with these changes is not just about compliance; it's about staying relevant and capable in a rapidly evolving professional landscape.

Real-World Implications: For example, consider the impact of the IAASB's standards on a UK company's cross-border operations. The uniformity in audit approach facilitated by these standards means that the company's financial statements are readily accepted and understood in different jurisdictions, easing their path in global markets.

Case Studies and Research: Various studies, such as those published in academic journals on auditing, often highlight the effectiveness of IAASB standards in enhancing audit quality. These studies serve as a testament to the practical value of these standards in real-world scenarios.

FRC Scope and Authority of Audit and Assurance Pronouncements

The Financial Reporting Council (FRC) in the United Kingdom plays a pivotal role in setting the standards for audit and assurance. Understanding the scope and authority of their pronouncements is essential for anyone preparing for the ICAEW ACA UK Audit and Assurance examination. Let's delve into this subject in a detailed and approachable manner.

FRC's Scope in Audit and Assurance
Standards Setting: The FRC is responsible for developing and issuing auditing standards, ethical standards, and quality control standards for audits in the UK. This includes the overall framework within which auditors operate.

Public Interest Oversight: The FRC ensures that the audit process aligns with the public interest. This includes monitoring and promoting the relevance, reliability, and quality of information provided to investors and others.

Regulatory Role: The FRC also has a regulatory role, overseeing the conduct of professional accountants through its subsidiary bodies like the Audit Quality Review (AQR) team.

Authority of Audit and Assurance Pronouncements

Binding Nature: The pronouncements issued by the FRC are authoritative and binding on all auditors operating in the UK. Non-compliance can lead to sanctions or legal implications.

International Alignment: The FRC's standards often align with International Standards on Auditing (ISA), ensuring UK audits are globally respected and recognized.

Real-Life Application and Examples
Case Studies: Look at real-life cases where adherence to or deviation from FRC standards impacted audit outcomes. For instance, the collapse of Carillion plc highlighted the importance of stringent audit standards.

Regulatory Actions: Consider how FRC's regulatory actions, such as fines or sanctions against audit firms, reinforce the importance of these standards.

Technical Insights
Risk Assessment Standards: Understand how the FRC's standards guide auditors in assessing audit risk, a crucial element in the auditing process.

Ethical Standards: Delve into the FRC's ethical standards, especially in areas like auditor independence and conflict of interest.

Keeping Up-to-Date
Recent Changes: Stay informed about recent changes or updates to the FRC standards. For example, the post-Brexit scenario might bring changes in regulatory frameworks.

Continued Professional Development: Engage in CPD activities, including seminars and webinars that discuss FRC standards.

Examination Preparation Guide
Study Materials: Utilize official ICAEW study materials that cover FRC pronouncements in detail.

Practice Questions: Regularly practice exam questions that specifically focus on FRC's scope and authority.

Understanding vs Memorization: Aim to understand the principles behind the FRC's pronouncements rather than just memorizing them.

International Standards on Quality Management (Isqms) (UK)

Quality Management for Firms That Perform Audits or Reviews of Financial Statements, or Other Assurance or Related Services Engagements

Quality management for firms conducting audits, reviews of financial statements, or other assurance or related services engagements is a critical area, especially in the context of ICAEW (Institute of Chartered Accountants in England and Wales) ACA (Associate Chartered Accountant) UK Audit and Assurance standards.

1. Understanding Quality Management:
Quality management in the audit context refers to a firm's collective processes and actions to ensure that the services provided meet professional standards and regulatory requirements. It's not just about checking boxes; it's about fostering a culture of excellence and integrity. Imagine a tailor carefully measuring and stitching a suit to ensure a perfect fit; similarly, quality management in auditing is about precision and attention to detail.

2. Key Elements of Quality Management:

Leadership Commitment: Like a captain steering a ship, firm leadership must be committed to quality. This includes setting a tone at the top that values quality and integrity above all.
Ethical Requirements: Auditors must adhere to principles of integrity, objectivity, professional

competence, and confidentiality. It's akin to a doctor-patient relationship, where trust is paramount.
Acceptance and Continuance of Client Relationships: Firms should only take on or continue client relationships if they have the capability to perform the engagement and comply with ethical requirements. It's like a chef ensuring they have the right ingredients before starting a meal.
Human Resources: Ensuring the team has the right mix of knowledge, skills, and experience is crucial. Think of a football team where each player's skills are essential to winning the game.
Engagement Performance: This involves planning, supervising, and a review process. It's similar to a conductor leading an orchestra, where every note matters.
Monitoring: Regular checks and balances, like a gardener tending to a garden, ensure ongoing compliance and identify areas for improvement.
3. Real-Life Application:
A study by the American Accounting Association found that firms with robust quality management systems had significantly fewer audit deficiencies. This highlights the tangible benefits of a strong quality management system.

4. Importance in ICAEW ACA Exams:
For students preparing for the ICAEW ACA exams, understanding these principles is not just about passing a test. It's about laying the groundwork for a career defined by excellence and ethical practice. Imagine each exam topic as a tool in your toolkit, essential for building a successful career.

5. Continuous Improvement:
Quality management is not a one-time effort but a continuous journey. Firms must adapt to changes in regulations, standards, and the business environment, much like a sailor adjusting sails to changing winds.

6. Technology's Role:
Advancements in technology, like AI and data analytics, are reshaping the audit landscape. Embracing these tools can enhance quality and efficiency.

Engagement Quality Reviews

Engagement Quality Reviews (EQRs) are an essential aspect of the audit and assurance process, especially within the framework of the ICAEW ACA (Institute of Chartered Accountants in England and Wales, Associate Chartered Accountant) in the UK. These reviews aim to ensure the quality and integrity of an audit.

What is an Engagement Quality Review?
An Engagement Quality Review is a process where an independent reviewer, usually someone with extensive experience in auditing, examines an audit to ensure it meets the required standards of quality. The EQR process is particularly important in complex or high-risk audits, where there's a greater chance of error or oversight.

Key Components of an EQR
Reviewer Independence: The reviewer must not be part of the audit team and should have no conflict of interest. This independence ensures an unbiased review.

Review of Critical Audit Matters: The reviewer focuses on areas of the audit that are complex, subjective, or involve significant judgment. For instance, in an audit of a large corporation, the valuation of complex financial instruments would be a critical area.

Assessment of Conclusions: The EQR includes an evaluation of the audit team's conclusions. The reviewer must agree that the conclusions are supported by evidence and are consistent with the accounting framework.

Evaluation of Communication: The reviewer also examines how well the audit team communicated with the client's management and those charged with governance.

Real-Life Example
Consider the audit of a multinational corporation with diverse operations. The EQR might focus on how the audit team assessed the valuation of international assets, ensuring that the team considered the different economic and regulatory environments in which the assets are located.

Importance of EQRs in ICAEW ACA
For ACA students, understanding the EQR process is crucial. It's not just about checking an audit's accuracy; it's about ensuring the audit is performed with professional skepticism and adheres to ethical standards. This understanding is vital for passing exams and for practical auditing work.

Studies and Technical Knowledge
Research shows that EQRs significantly improve audit quality. A study by the Public Company Accounting

Oversight Board (PCAOB) found that audits with an EQR had fewer deficiencies compared to those without. This finding underscores the value of EQRs in enhancing audit reliability.

Best Practices for EQRs
Thorough Documentation: The reviewer should document their findings and the basis for their conclusions. This documentation is crucial for accountability and for future reference.

Timely Review: The EQR should be conducted in a timely manner, ideally parallel to the audit process, to ensure any issues can be addressed promptly.

Continual Training: Reviewers should undergo regular training to stay updated with the latest auditing standards and practices.

International Standards on Auditing (UK)

200 (Revised June 2016) (Updated May 2022) Overall Objectives of the Independent Auditor and the Conduct of an Audit in Accordance with International Standards on Auditing (UK)

The International Standards on Auditing (UK) (ISA (UK)), particularly the "Overall Objectives of the Independent Auditor and the Conduct of an Audit in Accordance with International Standards on Auditing (UK)," revised in June 2016 and updated in May 2022, play a crucial role in shaping the audit practices in the UK. These standards, relevant for students preparing for the ICAEW ACA exams in Audit and Assurance, offer a comprehensive framework for conducting high-quality audits that are consistent, reliable, and effective.

Key Objectives of an Independent Auditor
Obtain Reasonable Assurance: The auditor aims to obtain reasonable assurance about whether the financial statements as a whole are free from material misstatement, whether due to fraud or error. This provides a high level of certainty, though not absolute, due to inherent limitations in an audit.

Express an Opinion: The auditor expresses an opinion on whether the financial statements are prepared, in all material respects, in accordance with an applicable financial reporting framework.

Report on Financial Statements: Ensuring the financial statements are free from material misstatement and presenting the findings in a report.

Conducting an Audit in Accordance with ISA (UK) Compliance with Relevant Requirements: The auditor must comply with all relevant ethical requirements, including independence, and conduct the audit in accordance with ISAs (UK).

Professional Skepticism and Judgment: Auditors are required to exercise professional skepticism throughout the audit, questioning potential misstatements and making judgments based on evidence gathered.

Sufficient and Appropriate Evidence: Gathering enough appropriate evidence is vital to justify the auditor's conclusion and opinion on the financial statements.

Real-life Applications and Technical Knowledge
In real-world scenarios, auditors face various challenges. For instance, in the case of a large corporation, auditors must navigate complex financial transactions, assess risks of material misstatement due to fraud, and adapt their audit approach accordingly. This may involve using advanced audit technologies and analytical tools.

Updates in May 2022
The updates made in May 2022 focus on enhancing the clarity and applicability of standards in evolving audit environments. This includes considerations for new technologies, evolving financial and business practices, and increased emphasis on ethical principles.

Examination Preparation
For ICAEW ACA students, understanding these standards is crucial. It's not just about memorizing the standards, but understanding their application in various scenarios. Consider studying case studies where these standards have been applied in real audits. This will help in grasping the practical implications and applications of the standards.

210 (Revised June 2016) (Updated May 2022) Agreeing the Terms of Audit Engagements

Let's dive into ISA (UK) 210, "Agreeing the Terms of Audit Engagements," in a way that's fresh, imaginative, yet easy to grasp. Think of this as a roadmap for your journey into the world of auditing as per the ICAEW ACA standards.

1. The Heart of ISA (UK) 210: A Handshake in Words
Imagine ISA (UK) 210 as a handshake agreement, but in writing. It's like a promise between the auditor and the company being checked (let's call them 'the audited'). This promise explains what the audit will look into, and what both parties should expect from each other. It's all about avoiding surprises and being on the same page.

2. The Audit Engagement Letter: Your Audit's Blueprint
This letter is like a treasure map, guiding the auditor and the audited. It's a detailed guide that spells out the journey of the audit – what's the goal, what path will the auditor take, and what rules does the company need

to follow. Think of it as a contract that lays everything out clearly.

3. A Real-World Scenario: The Story of XYZ Ltd.
Picture a company, XYZ Ltd. They're about to be audited. The engagement letter they get is like a script for a play. It tells them what role they play (preparing accurate accounts) and what role the auditor plays (giving an honest opinion on those accounts).

4. When Things Change: The Art of Adaptation
Sometimes, the script needs rewrites. Maybe the company's story changes, or new rules come into play. ISA (UK) 210 is cool with that. It says, "Let's update our agreement and keep the show going." This flexibility is key in the dynamic world of business.

5. The Auditor's Role: A Detective with Principles
Auditors are like detectives with a strict moral code. They need to be independent, unbiased, and always on the lookout for clues that something might be wrong with the financial statements. They don't take everything at face value and are always questioning, always verifying.

6. The Reality of Limitations: Not All-Seeing, but Still Sharp
Auditing isn't about seeing every single detail. It's more like using a powerful magnifying glass to spot the important bits. Auditors can't check every transaction, but they're smart about what they inspect to catch any major errors.

7. For the Aspiring Auditors: Your Adventure Awaits
As you prepare to step into the world of auditing, remember ISA (UK) 210 is your foundational guide. It's

not just about rules and technicalities; it's about understanding the dance between auditors and businesses, and how to keep in step with each other.

220 (Revised July 2021) Quality Management for an Audit of Financial Statements

Understanding ISA 220 (Revised July 2021), titled "Quality Management for an Audit of Financial Statements", is crucial for any professional preparing for the ICAEW ACA UK Audit and Assurance examination. This standard outlines the responsibilities of an audit firm, specifically regarding the management of quality on audits of financial statements.

1. Firm's Responsibilities: ISA 220 emphasizes the audit firm's responsibility in establishing and maintaining a system of quality management. This system should be tailored to the nature and size of the firm, ensuring that audits are conducted in accordance with the standards and legal requirements. A real-life example is a small audit firm implementing different quality control procedures than a large multinational firm, due to differences in resources and the complexity of the audits.

2. Engagement Partner's Role: The standard highlights the role of the engagement partner. They must ensure that the audit is planned and performed in line with the firm's quality management policies and procedures. In practice, this means the partner is responsible for assembling a team with the necessary competencies and capabilities.

3. Ethical Requirements: Adherence to relevant ethical requirements, including independence, is a key focus. An audit team must be free from conflicts of interest, and there must be policies in place to monitor this. For instance, if an auditor has a financial interest in a client, this poses a threat to independence and must be addressed.

4. Acceptance and Continuance of Client Relationships: The standard dictates criteria for the acceptance and continuation of client relationships. This is crucial for maintaining integrity and professionalism in the audit. Firms should evaluate whether they have the skills and resources to undertake the audit and whether the client complies with ethical requirements.

5. Assignment of Engagement Teams: Selecting a team with the appropriate competencies and capabilities for the audit task is vital. This includes considering the complexity of the audit, the team's understanding of relevant industries, and technical knowledge.

6. Direction, Supervision, and Performance: The standard requires that the audit be properly directed, supervised, and performed in compliance with professional standards. This involves regular reviews of work, ensuring the team understands their responsibilities, and maintaining a dialogue with the client.

7. Monitoring and Remediation: There should be a process to monitor the overall effectiveness of the quality management system, with remediation where necessary. This could include reviewing a sample of audit engagements to ensure compliance with standards and identifying areas for improvement.

230 (Revised June 2016) (Updated May 2022) Audit Documentation

Audit documentation, often referred to as "working papers" or "workpapers", is a crucial component in the audit process. It serves as a record of the evidence gathered by auditors to support their opinion on the financial statements. In the context of the ICAEW ACA UK Audit and Assurance, understanding the principles of audit documentation, as outlined in ISA 230 (Revised June 2016, Updated May 2022), is vital for any aspiring auditor.

Understanding ISA 230 - Audit Documentation
ISA 230 outlines the auditor's responsibilities for preparing audit documentation in an audit of financial statements. The main objectives of this standard are to:

Provide a Record of the Basis for the Audit Report: Audit documentation should provide a clear understanding of the work done, evidencing a quality audit.
Enable an Experienced Auditor to Understand: It should be sufficiently detailed to allow an experienced auditor, who has had no previous connection with the audit, to understand the work performed.
Key Components of Audit Documentation
Nature, Timing, and Extent of Audit Procedures: This includes documentation of the rationale for the audit approach, the timing of the audit, and the nature and extent of audit procedures performed.
Audit Evidence: Records of the audit evidence gathered and the conclusions the auditor has drawn from this evidence.

Audit Conclusion: The documentation should clearly show how the auditor arrived at the overall conclusion and how it supports the auditor's report.

Real-Life Examples

Consider a scenario where an auditor is assessing a company's inventory. The auditor will document the process of physically verifying inventory, reconciling it with the company's records, and evaluating the company's method of inventory valuation. These documents serve as evidence that the auditor has performed due diligence.

Technical and Rare Knowledge

Electronic Documentation: With advancements in technology, auditors increasingly use electronic audit documentation methods. This includes using software for sampling and analysis, and storing documents electronically.

Professional Skepticism: Documenting instances where professional skepticism was applied is a subtle but critical part of audit documentation.

Studies and Research

Research has shown that well-maintained audit documentation improves the quality of audits. A study published in the 'Accounting Review' indicated that detailed documentation leads to better decision-making in the audit process.

240 (Revised May 2021) (Updated May 2022) The Auditor's Responsibilities Relating to Fraud in an Audit of Financial Statements

The Auditor's Responsibilities Relating to Fraud in an Audit of Financial Statements, as revised in May 2021 and updated in May 2022, are crucial aspects of the ICAEW ACA UK Audit and Assurance. Understanding these responsibilities is not just about memorizing rules; it's about recognizing the real-world implications of fraud in financial reporting and how auditors play a pivotal role in detecting and preventing it. Let's explore this in detail, keeping in mind the need for simple language and practical examples.

1. Understanding Fraud
Fraud in financial statements can take many forms, such as falsifying records or intentionally omitting transactions. Auditors need to be vigilant, as their role is not to detect all frauds but to identify material misstatements due to fraud. It's like being a detective in the world of numbers, where even a small clue can reveal a bigger picture.

2. Professional Skepticism
Auditors must approach their work with a mindset of professional skepticism. This means always questioning the evidence and not taking things at face value.

3. Risk Assessment
Auditors are required to assess the risk of material misstatement due to fraud. This involves understanding the client's business, the environment they operate in, and the quality of their internal control systems. It's akin to assessing the safety of a building; you need to

check the foundations, the materials used, and the overall structure.

4. Gathering Evidence

Collecting evidence is a critical step. Auditors must ensure that the evidence gathered is sufficient and appropriate. This can involve a range of activities, from interviewing staff to scrutinizing financial records. It's like putting together pieces of a puzzle to see the full picture.

5. Responding to Detected Fraud

If fraud is detected, auditors must respond appropriately. This could mean expanding the scope of the audit or informing those charged with governance. It's a responsibility that requires both tact and firmness.

6. Communication

Auditors are also responsible for communicating about fraud. This includes discussing with the management and those charged with governance the risks of material misstatement due to fraud.

7. Documentation

Finally, auditors must thoroughly document their findings, the rationale for their decisions, and how they addressed the risk of fraud in their audit.

Real-Life Example

Consider the case of a large corporation where an auditor noticed discrepancies in inventory records. By applying professional skepticism and conducting a thorough examination, the auditor discovered a scheme where inventory was being overstated to inflate the company's financial health. This led to significant changes in the company's financial statements and internal controls.

250 Section A (Revised November 2019) (Updated May 2022) Consideration of Laws and Regulations in an Audit of Financial Statements

Section A (Revised November 2019) (Updated May 2022) of the ICAEW ACA UK Audit and Assurance guide focuses on the consideration of laws and regulations in an audit of financial statements. This is a critical area for auditors, as it involves understanding and evaluating the impact of legal and regulatory frameworks on the financial statements of an audited entity. Let's delve into this topic in a detailed and accessible manner, suitable for an examination preparation guide.

Understanding Laws and Regulations in Audits
1. Identifying Relevant Laws and Regulations: Auditors must first identify the laws and regulations that are relevant to the financial statements. These might include tax laws, environmental regulations, and employment laws. Real-life examples include the impact of GDPR on data handling and financial reporting or the implications of environmental regulations on a company's asset valuation.

2. Assessing Compliance: Auditors must assess whether the entity has complied with these laws and regulations. Non-compliance can lead to financial penalties, which must be reflected in the financial statements. For instance, a study by the University of Oxford highlighted how financial penalties for non-compliance

with environmental laws significantly affected the financial statements of several major corporations.

3. Materiality of Non-Compliance: It is crucial to determine the materiality of any non-compliance. Materiality in this context means the significance of non-compliance on the financial statements. For example, minor labor law violations might not be material, but major environmental law breaches could be.

Reporting Obligations
1. Communicating with Governance: If significant non-compliance is identified, auditors must communicate this to the entity's governance structures, like the board of directors or audit committee.

2. External Reporting: In some cases, auditors may have a legal obligation to report non-compliance to external authorities. This decision depends on the nature of the non-compliance and the legal framework in which the audit is conducted.

3. Impact on Auditor's Report: Non-compliance can impact the auditor's report, leading to a qualified opinion or an emphasis of matter paragraph if the issue is material but does not pervade the entire set of financial statements.

Real-Life Implications
For example, a study by the Financial Reporting Council (FRC) in the UK showed that companies often face challenges in complying with new accounting standards and regulations, impacting their financial statements and the audit process. An auditor's

awareness and understanding of these changes are crucial.

260 (Revised November 2019) (Updated May 2022) Communication with Those Charged with Governance

ISA 260, titled "Communication with Those Charged with Governance," is a crucial component in the audit process, as outlined by the International Standards on Auditing. Its revisions as of November 2019 and updates in May 2022 reflect the evolving nature of the auditing landscape. Understanding ISA 260 is essential for anyone preparing for the ICAEW ACA qualification in Audit and Assurance in the UK. Let's delve into its key aspects in a detailed and easy-to-understand manner.

Understanding ISA 260
Purpose of ISA 260: This standard emphasizes effective communication between auditors and those responsible for governance (like board members or audit committees). It ensures that significant audit matters are conveyed and understood, aiding in the transparency and efficiency of the audit process.

Who is Involved: The "those charged with governance" typically refers to individuals or groups (like audit committees) responsible for overseeing the strategic direction of the entity and obligations related to the accountability of the entity. This includes overseeing the financial reporting process.

Key Matters of Communication: The auditor must communicate specific points, such as the scope and timing of the audit, significant audit findings, and any deficiencies in internal controls that they identify during the audit.

Practical Application in Real Life
Example Scenario: Imagine an audit of a large corporation where the auditor discovers inconsistencies in financial reporting. Under ISA 260, the auditor is obligated to report these findings to the audit committee, explaining the potential impact on the financial statements and the need for corrective action.

Impact of Effective Communication: Effective implementation of ISA 260 can lead to a better understanding of potential financial risks, improved financial reporting, and strengthened internal controls.

The 2019 Revision and 2022 Update
2019 Revision: Introduced more clarity on the auditor's responsibility to communicate key audit matters and the judgment involved in these communications. It aims to enhance the quality and effectiveness of the communication.

2022 Update: Focused on aligning the standard with recent changes in auditing practices and the evolving nature of business and governance structures. It might include aspects like digital transformation impacts and emerging risks.

Tips for Examination Preparation
Understand the Essence: Focus on grasping the purpose and scope of ISA 260. Remember, it's about effective communication between auditors and governance bodies.

Real-life Cases: Review case studies or real audit scenarios where ISA 260 played a crucial role. This will help in understanding its application in real-world settings.

Updates and Revisions: Stay updated with the latest revisions and updates. Examiners often focus on recent changes to test your current knowledge.

Mock Communications: Practice writing mock communications to a fictional governance body based on different audit findings. This will help you understand how to effectively convey significant matters.

Stay Informed: Keep abreast of the latest in auditing standards and practices. This not only prepares you for the exam but also for a career in audit and assurance.

265 (Updated May 2022) Communicating Deficiencies in Internal Control to Those Charged with Governance and Management

Communicating deficiencies in internal control to those charged with governance and management is a critical aspect of the audit process, especially in the context of ICAEW's ACA UK Audit and Assurance. This process involves identifying and reporting weaknesses in a company's internal control system to its senior management and board members. Let's explore this concept in detail, keeping it simple, relevant, and practical.

Understanding Deficiencies in Internal Control
A deficiency in internal control is a flaw in the design or operation of a control that does not allow management or employees to prevent or detect and correct misstatements on a timely basis. Identifying these deficiencies is a fundamental part of an auditor's role. For instance, if a company lacks proper authorization procedures for expenditures, this could lead to unauthorized or fraudulent spending.

Communicating with Governance and Management
Once identified, these deficiencies must be communicated effectively. This is not just a bureaucratic step but a crucial part of ensuring the integrity of financial reporting. A real-life example could be a retail company where auditors found that cash handling procedures were not properly followed. The auditors would then need to report this to the company's management and board, explaining the risks and potential consequences.

The Role of ICAEW's ACA in Audit and Assurance
The ICAEW's ACA qualification emphasizes the importance of this communication. It trains auditors not only to identify and assess the significance of deficiencies but also to articulate them clearly and constructively. The goal is to encourage proactive steps towards rectification and improvement.

Categories of Deficiencies
Deficiencies are often categorized as either a 'significant deficiency' or a 'material weakness'. The former indicates a more severe problem that requires immediate attention. For example, if a financial institution lacks robust measures to prevent money laundering, this is a significant deficiency with legal and reputational implications.

Reporting and Documentation
Effective reporting involves not just stating the problem but also suggesting possible solutions. This can include recommendations for new controls or changes to existing procedures. Auditors must document their findings and communications comprehensively, as this forms a part of the audit trail and is essential for accountability and transparency.

Practical Implications
In practice, this process can be challenging. Auditors must balance the need for thoroughness with the need to maintain a constructive relationship with the client. It's about finding the right tone and approach - firm but fair, and always with the aim of improving the company's control environment.

Case Studies and Research

Studies have shown that effective communication of internal control deficiencies can lead to significant improvements in a company's operations. Research published in the Accounting Review indicated that companies often take corrective actions post-audit, leading to enhanced control mechanisms and reduced risk of fraud.

300 (Revised June 2016) (Updated May 2022) Planning an Audit of Financial Statements

Planning an audit of financial statements is an intricate and critical process, essential for maintaining the integrity and reliability of financial information. The guidelines and standards for this process have been updated over time, with notable revisions in June 2016 and further updates in May 2022. As part of the ICAEW ACA UK Audit and Assurance curriculum, understanding these updates is crucial for examination preparation. Here, we'll delve into this topic in a detailed, easy-to-understand manner, incorporating real-life examples and referencing studies where relevant.

1. Understanding Audit Standards and Regulations
The first step in planning an audit involves a thorough understanding of the relevant audit standards, such as International Standards on Auditing (ISA), and regulations specific to the UK context. The 2016 revision emphasized the importance of aligning audit practices with global standards, while the 2022 update brought in nuances specific to emerging financial challenges and technologies.

For example, a study by the Audit Quality Forum emphasized the need for auditors to be more skeptical and inquisitive, especially in complex financial environments.

2. Client Acceptance and Continuance
Auditors must assess whether to accept or continue with a client. This involves understanding the client's business, industry, and associated risks. The updated guidelines stress the importance of evaluating the

integrity of the client's management and their commitment to fair financial reporting.

A real-life example of this is when KPMG declined to continue as the auditor for a high-profile client due to concerns over financial irregularities, showcasing the practical application of these standards.

3. Risk Assessment and Materiality
A pivotal aspect of audit planning is assessing risks and determining materiality levels. The revisions have brought in a more dynamic approach to risk assessment, factoring in changes in the client's business environment, operations, and internal controls. It's about identifying areas where financial statements might be materially misstated.

For instance, the collapse of Carillion highlighted the need for auditors to have a robust risk assessment process, especially in assessing the viability of large contracts and commitments.

4. Audit Strategy and Plan
Developing an audit strategy tailored to the specifics of the client's business is crucial. This involves deciding on the nature, timing, and extent of audit procedures. The latest updates put greater emphasis on technology's role in auditing, encouraging the use of data analytics and other digital tools.

A study by the Financial Reporting Council (FRC) indicated that firms employing advanced data analytics in audits tend to have more robust audit quality controls.

5. Documentation and Quality Control
Proper documentation of the audit plan and ensuring quality control throughout the audit process are vital. The updates underscore the need for comprehensive documentation that reflects the auditor's understanding of the client and audit approach, along with evidence of review and supervision.

6. Ethics and Professional Skepticism
Maintaining high ethical standards and professional skepticism throughout the audit is paramount. The revisions reinforce the need for auditors to remain impartial and question evidence critically.

For example, the Enron scandal serves as a stark reminder of the consequences when auditors lose objectivity and skepticism.

315 (Revised July 2020) Identifying and Assessing the Risks of Material Misstatement

The topic of identifying and assessing the risks of material misstatement, as per ISA 315 (Revised July 2020), is a cornerstone in the field of audit and assurance, especially within the framework of the ICAEW ACA qualification in the UK. This standard plays a crucial role in guiding auditors to understand and evaluate risks in an audit engagement. Let's delve into this subject in a detailed and engaging manner, suitable for an examination preparation guide.

Understanding Material Misstatement Risks
Material misstatement risks are essentially the risks that financial statements might be significantly misstated due to error or fraud. As an auditor, you need to identify these risks to plan your audit accordingly. This involves understanding the entity, its environment, and its internal control.

1. Entity and Its Environment
Industry Understanding: Know the industry in which the entity operates. For instance, a tech company might face different risks compared to a manufacturing firm. Regulatory Framework: Be aware of the legal environment. For example, a pharmaceutical company must comply with health and safety regulations. Operational Characteristics: Understand the entity's operational specifics - how it generates and records transactions.
2. Entity's Internal Control
Assess the effectiveness of internal controls. Weak controls might increase the risk of misstatement.

Assessing Risk Factors

1. Transaction-Level Risks

Look at complex or unusual transactions. For example, a company entering a new market may have unfamiliar and risky transactions.

2. Fraud Risks

Consider the likelihood of fraud. This includes both management fraud and employee fraud.

3. Changes in Operations

Significant changes in operations can be a red flag. For instance, a sudden expansion or downsizing could impact financial reporting.

Practical Application

1. Real-Life Examples

Consider the case of a company overstating its inventory. This could be a risk if there's a lack of proper inventory controls.

A real-life example is the Enron scandal, where the company's financial health was grossly misstated.

2. Case Studies

Studies, such as those on financial scandals, often reveal common areas of risk misstatement, such as overstated assets or understated liabilities.

Key Considerations for Auditors

Professional Skepticism: Always approach an audit with a questioning mind.

Documentation: Record your risk assessment process meticulously.

Continual Assessment: Risks can change over the audit period. Regularly reassess them.

320 (Revised June 2016) (Updated May 2022) Materiality in Planning and Performing an Audit

Materiality in planning and performing an audit, as outlined in ISA 320 (Revised June 2016) and updated in May 2022, is a critical concept for auditors, particularly those preparing for the ICAEW ACA UK Audit and Assurance exams. Understanding this concept is not just about memorizing standards; it's about applying them in real-world scenarios. Let's delve into this in a way that's engaging, informative, and relevant.

1. Concept of Materiality:
At its core, materiality is about significance. In an audit context, it's about determining what is significant enough to influence the decisions of those relying on financial statements. Imagine a large company forgetting to record a small expense. This might be immaterial for a multi-million corporation, but for a small business, even a few hundred pounds could be material. Thus, materiality is relative.

2. Planning the Audit:
When planning an audit, the auditor must decide what level of inaccuracies or omissions would be considered material. This requires judgment and understanding of the client's business. For example, a retailer might focus on inventory levels, while a law firm might focus on receivables. Real-life scenarios, like a retailer during the holiday season, can greatly influence what is considered material.

3. Performing the Audit:
During the audit, the auditor uses the materiality threshold to evaluate findings. If errors below this threshold are found, they might be deemed acceptable. However, if errors are above the threshold, further investigation is needed. This approach ensures auditors focus their efforts on significant areas, improving efficiency.

4. Qualitative Materiality:
Materiality isn't just about numbers. Qualitative factors also play a role. For instance, even a small error that impacts a critical contract could be material if it affects stakeholder trust.

5. Revision and Adaptation:
The 2022 update to ISA 320 emphasizes the need for auditors to continually reassess materiality. Changes in the client's business, economic environment, or even during the audit itself, might require adjustments to what is considered material.

6. Application in Real Life:
Consider the case of a technology start-up. Initially, materiality might focus on revenue recognition, given its rapid growth. However, as it matures, materiality considerations might shift towards asset valuation.

7. Technical Knowledge:
For exam preparation, it's crucial to not just understand these concepts, but also to know how to apply them. Practice with case studies, stay updated with industry trends, and understand how different factors can influence materiality judgments.

8. Beyond the Exam:
Remember, the goal of understanding materiality in audits is not just to pass an exam but to become a proficient auditor who can make informed, ethical decisions in the complex world of finance.

330 (Revised July 2017) (Updated May 2022) The Auditor's Responses to Assessed Risks

The International Auditing and Assurance Standards Board (IAASB) revised ISA 330, "The Auditor's Responses to Assessed Risks," in July 2017, and it was updated again in May 2022. This standard provides guidance on how auditors should respond to risks they have identified and assessed during an audit. As you're preparing for the ICAEW ACA UK Audit and Assurance exams, it's crucial to understand this standard in detail. Let's break it down into simpler terms and explore real-life applications, ensuring the content is unique, creative, and tailored to examination preparation.

Understanding ISA 330
Risk Assessment and Link to Responses: ISA 330 mandates auditors to link their risk assessments to the design and implementation of their responses. This means that the responses should be directly proportional to the risk levels identified.

Designing and Implementing Audit Procedures: The standard requires auditors to design audit procedures that specifically address identified risks. This involves a mix of tests of controls (if the auditor plans to rely on them) and substantive procedures.

Material Misstatement: The procedures should be capable of detecting material misstatements at the assertion level. This could involve testing specific transactions or balances that are likely to be misstated.

Real-Life Application
Imagine you're auditing a company that has recently implemented a new financial software system. The risk of errors in financial reporting due to unfamiliarity with the new system is high. In response, you might increase the extent of substantive testing on transactions processed through this new system to catch potential misstatements.

Additional Considerations
Professional Skepticism: Always exercise professional skepticism. Even if controls seem robust, it's crucial to verify their effectiveness.

Documentation: ISA 330 also emphasizes the importance of documentation. Auditors must document their risk assessments and the basis for their conclusions about the sufficiency of the implemented audit procedures.

Responding to Higher Risks: For areas with higher assessed risks, such as areas prone to fraud, auditors should perform more extensive procedures.

Technical and Rare Knowledge
Using Technology in Audits: With advancements in technology, auditors can use data analytics to identify trends and anomalies in large datasets, providing a more robust response to assessed risks.
Understanding the Client's Business: Deep knowledge of the client's industry and business model can help tailor audit procedures more effectively.

402 (Updated May 2022) Audit Considerations Relating to an Entity Using a Service Organization

When delving into the topic of "Audit Considerations Relating to an Entity Using a Service Organization," as outlined in the ICAEW ACA UK Audit and Assurance guide (updated May 2022), it's essential to break down the 402 considerations into digestible, real-world applicable chunks. This exploration will not only prepare you for examinations but also enhance your practical understanding of audit processes in the context of service organizations.

Understanding the Context
Service Organization Dynamics: Service organizations are third-party entities that provide services to other entities (user entities). Examples include cloud service providers, payroll processing companies, and data centers. When a user entity outsources tasks or functions to a service organization, it introduces specific risks and complexities in the audit process.

Risk Assessment: A key audit consideration is understanding and assessing the risks associated with the service organization. This involves evaluating the nature of the services provided, the significance of the outsourced processes to the user entity's financial statements, and the control environment of the service organization.

Detailed Audit Considerations
A. Evaluating Internal Controls
Understanding Controls: Auditors must gain an understanding of how a user entity interacts with the

service organization and the controls implemented to monitor the effectiveness of the services provided.

Type 1 and Type 2 Reports: Service organizations often provide SOC 1 (Service Organization Control) reports. Type 1 reports evaluate the design of controls at a specific point in time, whereas Type 2 reports assess both the design and operating effectiveness of controls over a period.

B. Communication and Documentation
Communication with Service Organizations: Effective communication channels between the auditor, the user entity, and the service organization are crucial. This includes understanding the service organization's role and obtaining relevant documentation.

Contractual Agreements: Reviewing contracts or agreements between the user entity and the service organization can provide insights into the responsibilities and expectations.

C. Substantive Procedures
Testing Controls: If relying on the service organization's controls, auditors may need to perform tests of controls, particularly if there's no adequate Type 2 report.

Direct Substantive Testing: When controls cannot be relied upon, auditors may resort to more substantive testing of the transactions and balances related to the service organization.

Real-Life Application and Case Studies
Case Study – Payroll Processing: Consider a company outsourcing its payroll processing. The auditor would

need to understand the payroll service provider's controls over data accuracy and confidentiality, possibly reviewing SOC reports or performing independent tests.

Banking Sector Example: For a bank using a data center service organization, auditors would assess controls over data integrity, security, and disaster recovery plans.

Technical and Rare Knowledge Content Understanding SOC Reports: Gaining expertise in interpreting SOC 1 and SOC 2 reports is a specialized skill that auditors dealing with service organizations should develop.

Regulatory Considerations: Keeping abreast of changes in regulations, like GDPR for data protection, which impact service organizations and, by extension, the audit process, is crucial.

450 (Revised June 2016) (Updated May 2022) Evaluation of Misstatements Identified During the Audit

Evaluating misstatements identified during an audit is a crucial aspect of the audit process, especially in the context of the ICAEW ACA in the UK. The framework for this evaluation has been revised and updated over the years, most recently in May 2022. Let's dive into this topic, breaking it down into easily understandable parts, and incorporating real-life examples and technical insights.

1. Understanding Misstatements in Auditing
Definition: A misstatement in auditing refers to an error, either intentional (fraud) or unintentional (error), in the financial statements of a company. These can arise from various sources such as mistakes in gathering data, incorrect accounting estimates, or even oversight.
Example: Consider a company that incorrectly values its inventory due to an error in calculation. This leads to a misstatement in the financial statements.
2. Identification of Misstatements
Process: Auditors use various methods such as analytical procedures, tests of controls, and substantive tests to identify misstatements.
Real-Life Scenario: An auditor might notice that the sales revenue of a company has significantly increased compared to the previous year without a corresponding increase in market share or marketing efforts. This discrepancy could indicate a misstatement.
3. Evaluating the Materiality of Misstatements
Concept of Materiality: Not all misstatements significantly impact the financial statements. Materiality refers to the threshold above which a misstatement is considered significant enough to

influence the economic decisions of users of these statements.

Example: A small rounding error in a large corporation's financial statement may be considered immaterial, whereas the same error in a small business could be material.

4. Aggregating and Assessing the Impact of Misstatements

Aggregation: It involves summing up all identified misstatements to assess their cumulative impact.

Assessment: The auditor needs to determine whether the aggregate of these misstatements is material. This decision can affect the audit opinion.

5. Communicating Misstatements

To Management: Auditors must communicate all identified misstatements to the management, regardless of their materiality.

Adjustments: Management is then responsible for making the necessary adjustments. If management refuses to adjust material misstatements, this could lead to a qualified or adverse audit opinion.

6. Documentation

Record-Keeping: Auditors must document all identified misstatements, the reasoning behind the assessment of their materiality, and how they were communicated and resolved.

Case Study: An audit firm documented a significant misstatement related to revenue recognition, which led to a restatement of the financial statements and highlighted the importance of thorough documentation.

7. Updates in the Standards (Revised June 2016, Updated May 2022)

Changes in Thresholds: The updates may involve changes in the thresholds for materiality or the methods of aggregating misstatements.

Focus on Risk: Recent updates often emphasize risk-based approaches, where auditors focus more on areas with higher risks of material misstatements.

8. Real-World Implications and Case Studies

Enron Scandal: This case highlighted how overlooked misstatements can lead to massive financial disasters.

Learning from Mistakes: Case studies in audit textbooks often reflect on real-life scenarios where misstatement evaluation played a crucial role in the audit outcomes.

500 (Updated May 2022) Audit Evidence

As you embark on your journey through the ICAEW ACA's Audit and Assurance module, understanding the nuances of audit evidence is crucial. Audit evidence is the bedrock of an auditor's assessment of a company's financial statements. Let's delve into this subject with a focus on real-life examples, practical insights, and up-to-date methodologies.

Understanding Audit Evidence
Audit evidence is information used by auditors to decide whether the financial statements of an audited entity are presented fairly in all material respects. This evidence can come in various forms and sources.

Types of Audit Evidence
Physical Verification: Inspecting tangible assets like inventory or equipment. For example, auditors physically counting inventory in a warehouse to verify records.
Documentation: Reviewing documents, whether internal or external. This could be contracts, invoices, or bank statements.
Observations: Observing a process or procedure being performed by others, like watching the year-end inventory counting process.
Inquiries: Asking questions from knowledgeable sources within or outside the entity. This includes discussions with management and staff.
Confirmations: Seeking information from independent third parties. For instance, confirming account balances with banks or debtors.
Recalculations: Checking the mathematical accuracy of documents or records.

Quality Over Quantity

The ISA (International Standards on Auditing) 500 states that it's not just the volume but the quality of audit evidence that's important. This means focusing on relevant and reliable information. For instance, evidence obtained from an independent external source may carry more weight than that obtained internally.

Real-life Examples

Enron Scandal: Lack of proper audit evidence contributed to the downfall of Enron. The auditors failed to scrutinize the company's financial statements rigorously, leading to one of the biggest bankruptcies in history.

Lehman Brothers: In this case, the audit failed to uncover the use of 'Repo 105', a questionable accounting technique, highlighting the importance of scrutinizing the quality of audit evidence.

Updated Practices (Post May 2022)

With technological advancements, the nature of audit evidence has evolved. Auditors now use data analytics tools to analyze entire datasets rather than relying on sample-based testing. This approach enhances the accuracy and reliability of the audit evidence collected.

501 (Updated May 2022) Audit Evidence – Specific Considerations for Selected Items

The topic of "Audit Evidence – Specific Considerations for Selected Items" as outlined in the ICAEW ACA UK Audit and Assurance syllabus is extensive, covering various elements that are critical for anyone preparing for an examination in this field. This overview will touch upon several key areas within this subject, using simple language, real-life examples, and highlighting the importance of staying current with the latest standards and practices.

Understanding Audit Evidence
Audit evidence is the information gathered by auditors to conclude whether the financial statements of an entity are presented fairly. It's the cornerstone of an audit. The type and amount of evidence considered vary based on the auditor's assessment of the entity's risk.

Types of Audit Evidence
Physical Examination: This involves the physical inspection of tangible assets. For example, verifying the existence of a piece of machinery.
Documentation: Reviewing documents, whether in paper or electronic form, like invoices or contracts, to support transactions.
Observations: Observing a process or procedure being performed by others, like watching inventory counting.
Inquiries: Seeking information from knowledgeable sources within or outside the entity.
Recalculations: Checking the mathematical accuracy of documents or records.
Analytical Procedures: Evaluating financial information by studying plausible relationships among data.

Reperformance: Independent execution of procedures or controls originally performed as part of the entity's internal control.

Specific Considerations for Selected Items

Cash

Cash is a high-risk area due to its liquidity. Auditors often perform bank confirmations and review bank reconciliations to verify cash balances.

Inventory

Physical inventory counts are crucial. Auditors observe these counts and perform test counts to ensure accuracy.

Property, Plant, and Equipment (PPE)

Auditors assess depreciation methods, verify the existence of assets, and evaluate whether the assets are appropriately valued.

Investments

Reviewing investment policies, checking market values, and verifying ownership are key aspects.

Revenue

Auditors look at sales transactions near the end of the reporting period to ensure revenue is recorded in the correct period.

Payroll

Testing the payroll process, including wage rates and hours worked, is common to ensure accurate payroll recording.

Real-Life Example

Consider a retail company. An auditor might observe the inventory counting process, test a sample of transactions for revenue recognition, and examine loan agreements to verify interest expenses.

Importance of Staying Updated
Audit standards and practices constantly evolve. For instance, the shift towards more analytical procedures and the increased use of technology in audits is significant. Keeping abreast of these changes is crucial for exam success.

505 (Updated May 2022) External Confirmations

The ICAEW ACA UK Audit and Assurance section on External Confirmations, updated in May 2022, is a crucial component for anyone preparing for their examinations. This area is particularly important because it deals with the auditor's use of external confirmations as a part of the audit evidence-gathering process.

What are External Confirmations?

External confirmations refer to audit evidence obtained as a direct written response to the auditor from a third party (the confirmee), in paper form, or by electronic or other medium. The ISA 505 sets out the standards and guidance on using external confirmation procedures to obtain audit evidence. It's vital for audit and assurance students to understand that this process helps provide high-quality, reliable information directly from external sources.

Why are External Confirmations Important in Auditing?

Verification of Financial Information: External confirmations can verify account balances and other conditions. For example, confirming a bank balance with the bank helps ensure the accuracy of the reported financial position.

Evidence of Existence and Valuation: It's not just about numbers; external confirmations can also corroborate the existence of certain assets. For instance, confirming outstanding receivables through debtor confirmations.

Reducing Risk of Material Misstatement: By obtaining evidence from independent sources, auditors reduce the risk of material misstatement in financial statements.

How to Apply External Confirmations in Auditing?

Understanding the Entity and its Environment: Before sending out confirmations, it's crucial to understand the client's business environment. This knowledge guides the selection of items for confirmation.

Selecting Items for Confirmation: Not all items need confirmation. The auditor should use judgment to select significant items based on risk assessments.

Designing the Confirmation Request: The request should be clear and concise. It might ask for confirmation of a specific balance or request information about transactions.

Evaluating the Responses: Responses to confirmations should be critically evaluated. Non-responses or discrepancies need to be investigated further.

Real-Life Example and Studies

A study published in the 'Auditing: A Journal of Practice & Theory' examined the efficacy of audit confirmations. It found that confirmations are particularly effective in detecting fraud in financial statements, highlighting their importance in audit practice.

510 (Revised June 2016) Initial Audit Engagements - Opening Balances

Understanding ISA 510 (Revised June 2016) "Initial Audit Engagements - Opening Balances" is crucial for anyone preparing for the ICAEW ACA exams, particularly in the Audit and Assurance module. This standard is fundamental in guiding auditors on how to approach opening balances during the first audit of a company. Let's dive into its key elements in a comprehensive, yet straightforward manner, suitable for exam preparation.

Objective of ISA 510
The primary objective of ISA 510 is to establish standards and provide guidance on the auditor's responsibilities concerning opening balances in initial audit engagements. It focuses on:

The appropriateness of accounting policies reflected in the opening balances.
The consistency of the application of accounting policies with those of the current period.
Key Considerations
Audit Evidence for Opening Balances:

Auditors should gather sufficient appropriate audit evidence regarding the opening balances. This involves examining documentation from the previous year, such as audited financial statements and audit reports.
Real-life example: If a company had significant property acquisitions in the previous year, the auditor would review the related documentation to ensure proper valuation and recording.

Accounting Policies Consistency:

The auditor must assess whether the accounting policies used for opening balances are consistent with those applied in the current period. Any changes should be justified and properly disclosed.

For instance, if a company shifts from FIFO (First-In, First-Out) to LIFO (Last-In, First-Out) inventory accounting, this change needs a valid reason and adequate disclosure.

Material Misstatements:

Identifying material misstatements in opening balances is vital. These might result from errors or fraud in the previous period and can significantly impact the current period's financial statements.

Imagine a scenario where last year's revenue was overstated. This overstatement, if not corrected, will affect the current year's retained earnings.

Limitations Encountered:

If the auditor faces limitations in obtaining sufficient appropriate audit evidence concerning opening balances, this situation should be adequately reported. A real-life case could be an inability to confirm the existence of inventory carried forward from the previous year due to lost records.

Reporting Considerations

Qualified or Disclaimer of Opinion:

If the auditor concludes that the effect of misstated opening balances is material and has not been adequately presented or disclosed, a modification to the auditor's opinion on the financial statements may be necessary. This could be a qualified opinion or a disclaimer of opinion, depending on the situation's severity.

Practical Implications
New Auditor Challenges:

A new auditor might face challenges when the preceding year's audit was not performed, or the financial statements were audited by another auditor. In such cases, the new auditor must perform additional procedures to obtain confidence in the opening balances.

Impact on Audit Planning:

Understanding the implications of ISA 510 is crucial for audit planning. Auditors must allocate appropriate resources and time to scrutinize opening balances, especially in complex areas like long-term contracts or intangible assets.

Exam Preparation Tips
Understand Key Principles:

Focus on understanding the rationale behind the requirements of ISA 510. This helps in applying these principles to various scenarios in exam questions.

Practice with Real-Life Scenarios:

Use case studies or scenarios from real audit engagements to apply the principles of ISA 510. This not only prepares you for the exam but also for practical audit situations.

Stay Updated:

Always check for any updates or amendments to ISA 510, as auditing standards are subject to change and evolve with the business environment.

520 (Updated May 2022) Analytical Procedures

Analytical procedures are essential in the field of audit and assurance, especially for professionals preparing for the ICAEW ACA qualification in the UK. Understanding these procedures is crucial for auditors to assess the financial information of an organization effectively. While there are numerous analytical procedures, I'll focus on explaining the concept and providing some key examples, rather than listing all 520 updated procedures as of May 2022.

Understanding Analytical Procedures
1. Definition and Purpose:

Analytical procedures are used throughout the audit process, especially during planning and review stages. The main purpose is to identify the consistency and predictability of financial data, detect any unusual transactions or trends, and assess the business risks.
2. Types of Analytical Procedures:

Comparative Analysis: Comparing current financial statements with previous periods, budgets, or industry norms.
Trend Analysis: Looking at financial statements over several periods to identify patterns or trends.
Ratio Analysis: Using ratios like profitability, liquidity, solvency, and efficiency ratios to evaluate financial health.
Reasonableness Testing: Assessing whether financial data is reasonable based on other known data or industry benchmarks.

Real-Life Application Examples

1. Comparative Analysis in a Manufacturing Company:

An auditor might compare the cost of raw materials from one year to another. If there's a significant increase, it could indicate potential issues like supplier problems or theft.

2. Trend Analysis in Retail Business:

Auditors might review sales trends over several quarters. A consistent decline in sales could signal market issues or internal problems like poor product quality.

3. Ratio Analysis in Service Industry:

By analyzing profitability ratios, auditors might assess whether a service company is managing its expenses effectively compared to its revenue generation.

Practical Tips for ICAEW ACA Candidates

Deep Understanding of Business Context: Know the industry and business model of the entity you are auditing. This helps in making relevant and effective analytical comparisons.

Use of Technology: Leverage software tools for data analysis. These tools can efficiently handle large datasets and perform complex calculations.

Critical Thinking: Always question the results. If something seems off, it might warrant a deeper dive.

Communication: Be prepared to discuss your findings clearly, both in written reports and verbally.

Continuous Learning: Stay updated with industry trends, new accounting standards, and technological advancements.

Studies and Research
Various studies have shown the effectiveness of analytical procedures in auditing. For instance, research published in the "Auditing: A Journal of Practice & Theory" often provides insights into how analytical procedures can be used to detect financial statement fraud.

530 (Updated May 2022) Audit Sampling

Audit sampling is a fundamental concept in audit and assurance, particularly within the ICAEW ACA qualification in the UK. Understanding the 530 standard, updated in May 2022, is crucial for any aspiring auditor. The purpose of audit sampling is to provide a reasonable basis for the auditor to draw conclusions about the population from which the sample is drawn.

Understanding Audit Sampling
Audit sampling involves applying audit procedures to less than 100% of items within an account balance or class of transactions. This approach helps auditors to make conclusions about the entire population by examining a subset of it, making the audit process more efficient.

ISA 530 - Audit Sampling
Objective: The main objective of ISA 530 is to establish principles and provide guidance on designing and selecting an audit sample and evaluating the sample results.

Applicability: It applies when the auditor has decided to use sampling in performing audit procedures.

Types of Sampling:

Statistical Sampling: It's often used because it allows the auditor to measure and control the sampling risk. Non-Statistical Sampling: Does not use probability theory but should be as representative as possible.

Sample Design, Size, and Selection:

The auditor should consider the specific audit objectives, the nature of the population, and the sampling and selection methods.

Evaluating Sample Results:

The auditor assesses the deviations and misstatements found in the sample to draw conclusions about the entire population.

Real-Life Application

Imagine an auditor working on the financial statements of a large retailer. They might be interested in testing the occurrence of sales transactions. Instead of examining every single sales transaction for the year, the auditor would select a sample. The selection might be random or based on certain criteria, such as high-value transactions.

Importance in Audit and Assurance

Effective sampling in auditing ensures that auditors can make reasonable conclusions without examining every item. This efficiency is vital in large-scale audits where examining every transaction or balance is impractical.

Challenges and Considerations

Sampling Risk: This is the risk that the sample is not representative of the population.

Non-Sampling Risk: Due to factors other than the sample size, like human error.

Continuous Development

The field of auditing is continuously evolving, and standards like ISA 530 are regularly updated. It's crucial for auditors to stay informed about these changes to ensure compliance and effectiveness in their audit practices.

540 (Revised December 2018) (Updated May 2022) Auditing Accounting Estimates, and Related Disclosures

Auditing accounting estimates and related disclosures, particularly under the guidelines of ISA 540 (Revised December 2018) and its update in May 2022, is a critical area in the ICAEW ACA UK Audit and Assurance curriculum. The understanding of this standard is not just about grasping the technicalities; it's about embedding a mindset that appreciates the complexities and judgments involved in preparing and auditing accounting estimates.

Understanding ISA 540: A Conceptual Overview
Nature of Accounting Estimates: They are inherently subjective. They involve judgments made by management about uncertain future events – like estimating the useful life of an asset or provisions for doubtful debts.

Challenges in Auditing Estimates: Auditors must navigate through uncertainties and management biases. The revised ISA 540 intensifies the focus on risk assessment and demands a more robust audit response to higher risk estimates.

Enhanced Risk Assessment: Auditors are required to understand how management makes the estimates and the data they use. It's about getting into the shoes of management to see the rationale behind the numbers.

Practical Examples
Impairment Testing of Goodwill: Consider a company assessing impairment of goodwill. The auditor must evaluate the methodologies used, like discounted cash

flows, and assess the reasonableness of the assumptions, such as growth rates and discount rates.

Provision for Warranty Expenses: Companies often estimate warranty expenses based on historical data. Auditors should scrutinize the trends and changes in product quality or customer complaints that might impact future costs.

Real-life Implications and Updates
Post-2018 revision, there's a stronger emphasis on professional skepticism. For instance, during the COVID-19 pandemic, auditors had to exercise heightened skepticism given the increased uncertainty in estimates like fair values of assets or expected credit losses.

Technical Insights
Assessment of Model Integrity: Auditors must now delve deeper into the models used for estimates, checking for mathematical accuracy and appropriateness.

Increased Emphasis on Disclosures: The updated ISA 540 requires auditors to pay closer attention to how estimates are disclosed in financial statements, ensuring transparency and clarity.

Examination Preparation Guide
Understand the 'Why': Don't just memorize the standards; understand why they exist. This helps in applying them practically.

Practice with Scenarios: Engage with case studies or real-life examples. This builds the ability to think critically and apply standards in varied situations.

Stay Updated: Given the dynamic nature of auditing standards, keeping abreast of updates and industry trends is crucial.

Develop Professional Skepticism: Cultivate an attitude of questioning and not taking things at face value.

550 (Updated May 2022) Related Parties

 In preparing for the ICAEW ACA UK Audit and Assurance exam, understanding the concept of "Related Parties" is crucial. As of May 2022, the term "Related Parties" refers to individuals or entities that have a particular connection with the entity being audited. These connections can influence the financial statements and require special attention during an audit.

Definition and Importance
Related Parties are defined under the UK accounting and auditing standards. They include, but are not limited to, family members of key management personnel, subsidiaries, associates, joint ventures, and key management personnel themselves. The importance of identifying related parties lies in the potential for these relationships to affect the financial reporting and decision-making processes within an entity.

Examples from Real Life
Consider a scenario where a company sells goods to a business owned by a family member of a director at a price lower than the market value. This transaction should be scrutinized during the audit because it might not have occurred under the same terms if it had been between unrelated parties.

Risks Associated with Related Parties
Related party transactions can pose several risks:

Overstatement of Assets or Revenue: Transactions may be used to inflate revenue or asset values.
Understatement of Liabilities: Obligations to related parties might be under-reported.

126

Inappropriate Disclosure: Not disclosing these relationships can mislead stakeholders about the true nature of the entity's financial position.

Auditor's Responsibilities

Auditors must:

Identify Related Parties: Use information from management, previous audits, and the entity's environment.

Examine Transactions: Assess whether transactions with related parties were conducted on terms similar to those with unrelated parties.

Evaluate Financial Statement Disclosure: Ensure that all related party transactions are properly disclosed according to the relevant financial reporting framework.

Real-World Application

In a real audit, an auditor discovered that a significant loan to a director was not disclosed in the financial statements. This revelation led to a re-evaluation of the company's financial health and necessary adjustments in the financial statements.

Challenges in Auditing Related Parties

Auditors face challenges like limited information, management reluctance to disclose relationships, and complex corporate structures that obscure these relationships.

Staying Updated

As an aspiring auditor, staying updated with the latest standards and guidelines issued by bodies like the ICAEW and understanding the complexities of related party transactions are key to effective auditing.

Regularly reading industry publications, participating in continued professional education, and following real-world cases are excellent ways to remain informed.

560 Subsequent Events

Subsequent Events in the context of ICAEW ACA UK Audit and Assurance are critical aspects that auditors must consider. They refer to events that occur between the balance sheet date and the date when the financial statements are authorized for issue. Understanding these events is crucial for ensuring the financial statements provide a true and fair view of the company's financial position.

1. Types of Subsequent Events:

Adjusting Events: These events provide evidence of conditions that existed at the balance sheet date. For example, if a lawsuit is settled after the year-end, but relates to conditions that existed before the year-end, this would require an adjustment to the financial statements.

Non-Adjusting Events: These events reflect conditions that arose after the balance sheet date. An example could be a major acquisition or loss of a key supplier that occurs after the year-end. While these do not lead to adjustments in the financial statements, they may require disclosure.

2. Auditor's Responsibilities:

Identify Subsequent Events: The auditor should review the entity's procedures for identifying subsequent events and consider the need for any additional procedures.

Evaluate Management's Process: Auditors must evaluate how management has identified and distinguished between adjusting and non-adjusting events.

Examine Documentation: Reviewing board minutes, examining latest interim financial statements, and discussing with management are key steps.

3. Real-Life Examples:

Case of Company A: After the balance sheet date, Company A lost a significant lawsuit that had been in progress for months. This event was an adjusting subsequent event since it related to conditions existing at the balance sheet date.

Case of Company B: Company B received significant investment after the year-end. This event is non-adjusting but important for disclosure to inform users of the financial statements about the company's improved financial position.

4. Challenges and Best Practices:

Determining the Cut-Off: Establishing whether an event should be considered adjusting or non-adjusting can be challenging. Auditors must rely on their judgment and the specifics of each case.

Documentation: Maintaining robust documentation of the evaluation process is critical for audit quality.

Communication with Management: Effective communication with management is essential in identifying and evaluating subsequent events.

5. Recent Trends and Updates:

With the advent of rapid technological changes and economic uncertainties, subsequent events have become increasingly complex. This requires auditors to be more vigilant and updated with current economic conditions.

570 (Revised September 2019) (Updated May 2022) Going Concern

"ISA 570 (Revised September 2019) (Updated May 2022) - Going Concern" is a pivotal standard in the ICAEW ACA UK Audit and Assurance curriculum. Its revision and update reflect the evolving nature of audit practices and the importance of the going concern concept in financial reporting.

Understanding Going Concern
The concept of 'going concern' is foundational in accounting. It assumes that a business will continue to operate for the foreseeable future, without the need for liquidation or significant downsizing. As an auditor, you must assess whether this assumption is appropriate for the business you are auditing.

Revisions in ISA 570
The 2019 revision of ISA 570 primarily emphasizes the auditor's responsibilities in relation to going concern. The updates in 2022 further clarify these responsibilities, especially in the wake of economic uncertainties like those caused by global events.

Key Areas of Focus

Enhanced Risk Assessment: The revised standard requires auditors to perform a more robust risk assessment process, considering all available information about the future, which impacts the going concern assumption.

Management's Use of the Going Concern Basis: You must evaluate management's process in using the going concern basis in accounting. This involves understanding their methods, data, and conclusion.

Material Uncertainties: Identifying material uncertainties related to events or conditions that may cast significant doubt on the entity's ability to continue as a going concern is crucial.

Reporting: The standard outlines the implications of these uncertainties on the auditor's report. If such uncertainties exist, the auditor's report should clearly disclose them.

Real-Life Examples
Consider a retail company facing severe liquidity issues. As an auditor, you would examine their financial statements, forecasts, and plans to evaluate the feasibility of continuing operations. Any indication of potential insolvency would require a thorough investigation and appropriate disclosure in your audit report.

Studies and Technical Knowledge
Studies have shown that auditors' assessments of going concern risks can significantly impact financial markets. For example, research published in the "Journal of Accounting Research" indicates that auditors' going concern opinions are closely watched by investors.

Practical Application in Exams
In an examination scenario, you might be given a case study where you need to apply these principles. You'll have to analyze the financial information provided, assess the management's rationale, identify any material

uncertainties, and decide how these should be reflected in the audit report.

580 (Updated May 2022) Written Representations

The ICAEW ACA qualification in the UK, particularly in the field of Audit and Assurance, encompasses a broad spectrum of knowledge and skills. One critical aspect of this domain is understanding the concept of "Written Representations," which as of May 2022, includes 580 different items. Here, we will delve into this topic, highlighting its importance in the auditing process and providing real-life examples to illustrate the concepts more clearly.

What are Written Representations?
Written Representations are statements made by management or those charged with governance to the auditor, concerning specific aspects of the financial statements or related controls. These representations are an essential part of the evidence an auditor gathers during an audit, but they are not a substitute for other audit evidence that the auditor may gather.

Importance in Audit and Assurance
Confirmation of Information: They confirm information that is relevant to the financial statements, which the auditor has gathered during the audit.
Responsibility of Management: These representations underline the responsibility of management for the accuracy and completeness of the information in the financial statements.

Audit Evidence: They often serve as crucial audit evidence, especially for matters that do not leave a substantial audit trail.

Examples of Written Representations

Financial Statement Accuracy: A representation that all transactions have been recorded and are reflected in the financial statements.

Completeness of Information: Confirmation that all relevant information has been provided to the auditor.

Compliance with Laws and Regulations: Statement from management that the entity has complied with all applicable laws and regulations.

Real-Life Scenario

Imagine an audit of a large corporation. The auditor, in assessing the company's revenue recognition policies, would request a written representation from management confirming that all revenue recognized during the period met the relevant criteria for recognition and that there were no unrecorded revenues.

Technical and Rare Knowledge

Fraud Related Representations: In light of high-profile accounting scandals, auditors now frequently require representations specifically related to fraud, including the absence of unrecorded transactions or undisclosed related party transactions.

Use of Estimates: Representations about the fair presentation of estimates and the related methodological choices, especially in complex areas like impairment testing or valuation of financial instruments.

Studies and Research

Research in audit practice consistently shows the value of written representations as a means of mitigating risks associated with information asymmetry between the auditor and management. For instance, a study published in the "Journal of Accountancy" highlighted how auditors use these representations to cross-verify information and as a final check before issuing the audit opinion.

600 (Revised September 2022) Special Considerations – Audits of Group Financial Statements (including the Work of Component Auditors)

The ISA 600 "Special Considerations—Audits of Group Financial Statements (Including the Work of Component Auditors)" is a crucial part of the ICAEW ACA UK Audit and Assurance syllabus. This standard addresses how an auditor handling the audit of a group (the group engagement team) should consider the work of other auditors who audit the financial information of the components within the group.

Understanding ISA 600 is vital for anyone pursuing a career in audit and assurance in the UK. This standard is not just about the technicalities of auditing but also about the dynamics of working in a group audit setting. Let's break down the key elements in simple terms.

1. Understanding the Group Structure
A group audit involves multiple components - subsidiaries, divisions, or branches, possibly in different locations or countries. The group engagement team needs a thorough understanding of the group's structure and operations. This includes knowing the significance of different components and how they contribute to the group's financial statements.

2. Involvement with Component Auditors

The group engagement team often relies on the work of component auditors. It's essential for the group auditor to assess the competence and capabilities of these component auditors. This assessment helps in determining the extent of reliance that can be placed on their work.

3. Risk Assessment

One of the critical areas in group audits is the assessment of risk, especially the risk of material misstatement. The group engagement team needs to identify and assess risks specific to the group. This involves understanding how activities and controls at a component level affect the group's risks.

4. Communication

Effective communication between the group engagement team and component auditors is crucial. This includes clear instructions to component auditors about the audit's scope, areas of significant risk, and timelines.

Real-Life Example

The group auditor, based in the UK, must understand the different accounting practices and legal requirements in each country. They should communicate effectively with local auditors, ensuring that each component's audit aligns with the group audit's objectives.

Technical Considerations

Group audits can be complex, particularly when dealing with different accounting frameworks or when components are significant to the group. The group engagement team must have the technical skills to understand these complexities and integrate the work of component auditors effectively.

Ethical Considerations
Maintaining independence and objectivity is vital in group audits. The group engagement team should ensure that component auditors are independent and that their work does not compromise the overall audit quality.

610 (Revised June 2013) (Updated May 2022) Using the Work of Internal Auditors

ISA 610 (Revised 2013, Updated May 2022), "Using the Work of Internal Auditors," is a significant guideline in the ICAEW ACA UK Audit and Assurance syllabus. It provides detailed instructions on how external auditors can use the work of internal auditors to enhance the effectiveness and efficiency of the audit. Here's an examination preparation guide for understanding ISA 610 in the simplest English language, incorporating real-life examples, studies, and technical insights.

Understanding ISA 610
Purpose: ISA 610 assists external auditors in determining whether, and to what extent, to use the work of internal auditors. This can include using internal auditors to perform audit procedures or using their work as audit evidence.

Criteria for Use: The external auditor must evaluate the internal audit function's objectivity, technical competence, and whether they apply a systematic and disciplined approach, including quality control.

Cooperation and Coordination: Effective communication between external and internal auditors is vital. They should discuss audit plans and coordinate efforts to enhance efficiency and avoid duplication of efforts.

Real-Life Examples
A Retail Chain Case: In a large retail chain, the external auditor used the work of internal auditors who had

performed inventory counts and internal control testing. The external auditor evaluated the competence and objectivity of the internal audit team and concluded their work was reliable for audit purposes.

Banking Sector Example: In a bank audit, the external auditor may rely on internal auditors' assessments of loan provisioning and compliance with regulatory requirements, after ensuring that the internal auditors are independent from the bank's management.

Studies and Technical Insights
Research Findings: Studies have shown that when external auditors effectively use the work of internal auditors, it can lead to more efficient audits and potentially lower audit fees due to reduced duplication of work.

Technical Aspect: The external auditor must assess the risk of material misstatement in the financial statements and use that assessment to decide the extent to which they can rely on the work of internal auditors.

Applying ISA 610 in Audits
Evaluation Process: Assess the internal audit function's independence, scope of work, technical skills, and adherence to professional standards.
Communication: Establish clear communication channels with the internal audit team. Discuss the audit plan and understand the internal audits completed.
Documentation: Document the evaluation of the internal audit function and the rationale for using their work.

620 (Revised November 2019) (Updated May 2022) Using the Work of an Auditor's Expert

Understanding ISA 620 (Revised November 2019, Updated May 2022) - "Using the Work of an Auditor's Expert" - is crucial for anyone preparing for the ICAEW ACA UK Audit and Assurance examination. Let's break it down in simple terms with real-life examples and technical insights.

1. The Essence of ISA 620:
ISA 620 deals with the auditor's responsibility when using the work of an individual or organization in a field of expertise other than accounting or auditing, to assist the auditor in obtaining sufficient appropriate audit evidence. This could be a valuation expert, an actuary, or even a legal advisor.

Real-Life Example:
Imagine an audit involving a company that owns complex financial instruments. The auditor might not have deep expertise in valuing these instruments. Therefore, they would engage a financial instruments expert to provide the necessary insight.

2. Auditor's Responsibility:
The auditor must always remain responsible for the audit opinion. This means they cannot simply accept the expert's findings without applying professional skepticism. The auditor needs to understand the methods and assumptions used by the expert and ensure they are reasonable.

Example:
If an actuary is used to assess pension liabilities, the auditor should understand how the actuary arrived at their figures, including the assumptions about interest rates and employee lifespan.

3. Assessing the Expert:
ISA 620 requires auditors to assess the expert's objectivity, competence, and capability. This includes considering the expert's reputation, experience, and any potential conflicts of interest.

4. Documentation:
The auditor must document the nature, timing, and extent of the work, including the basis for the auditor's conclusion that the work is adequate for audit purposes.

5. Updated Elements in May 2022:
The May 2022 updates might include enhanced guidelines on how to assess the competence and capabilities of the expert, considering the evolving nature of certain fields of expertise.

Technical Insight:
In the era of Big Data and AI, auditors might increasingly rely on data science experts. Understanding how these experts process and analyze large datasets is becoming an important skill for auditors.

6. Examination Preparation Tips:

Understand the Standard:
Read ISA 620 thoroughly and understand its principles. Focus on the objectives and requirements of the standard.

Real-world Applications:
Think about how you would apply these principles in real audit scenarios. This will help you answer application-based questions.
Stay Updated:
Ensure you are aware of any recent updates or amendments to the standard.

700 (Revised November 2019) (Updated May 2022) Forming an Opinion and Reporting on Financial Statements

"Forming an Opinion and Reporting on Financial Statements" under ISA (International Standard on Auditing) 700, which was revised in November 2019 and updated in May 2022, is a critical component in the field of auditing, especially within the context of the ICAEW ACA (Institute of Chartered Accountants in England and Wales, Associate Chartered Accountant) qualification in the UK. This standard is pivotal for auditors as it provides the framework for forming an opinion on financial statements and how that opinion should be articulated in the audit report.

Understanding ISA 700
1. The Objective: The primary objective of ISA 700 is to ensure auditors express an appropriate opinion on whether financial statements are prepared in all material respects according to the applicable financial reporting framework. This ensures reliability and credibility in the financial statements, which is essential for stakeholders like investors, creditors, and others who rely on these reports for decision-making.

2. Forming an Opinion: The auditor needs to conclude, based on the audit evidence obtained, whether the financial statements as a whole are free from material misstatement. This involves a rigorous process of evidence gathering, risk assessment, and evaluation of the financial statements against the reporting framework, such as IFRS (International Financial Reporting Standards) or GAAP (Generally Accepted Accounting Principles).

3. Reporting: Once an opinion is formed, it must be clearly communicated through the audit report. ISA 700 stipulates the structure and content of this report, ensuring consistency and clarity in communication to users of the financial statements.

Real-World Application
In practice, auditors apply ISA 700 by thoroughly understanding the entity's operations, internal controls, and the financial reporting framework. For instance, an auditor of a UK-based company would need to be well-versed in UK GAAP or IFRS, depending on which framework the company uses.

A real-life example can be drawn from the audit of a large retail company. The auditor, after evaluating the company's inventory valuation methods and sales recognition policies, found them compliant with the applicable financial reporting standards. This evaluation, along with other audit procedures, formed the basis for expressing an opinion that the financial statements were free from material misstatement.

Challenges and Solutions
A significant challenge in applying ISA 700 is the increasing complexity of business transactions and financial reporting standards. Auditors must continually update their knowledge and skills. In response, training programs and continuous professional development are essential, as emphasized by ICAEW.

Examination Preparation Tips
Understand the Standard: Read ISA 700 thoroughly, focusing on the objectives, requirements, and application material.

Practical Examples: Engage with case studies that apply ISA 700 in different scenarios. This helps in understanding the standard's application in real-life contexts.

Stay Updated: Keep abreast of any changes or updates to the standard, as auditing is a dynamic field with frequent updates.

Mock Audits: Practice by conducting mock audits or reviewing audit reports. This provides practical experience in forming opinions and reporting.

Discussion Groups: Join study groups or discussion forums to share knowledge and clarify doubts.

Critical Thinking: Develop critical thinking and analytical skills to assess different audit situations effectively.

701 (Revised November 2019) (Updated May 2022) Communicating Key Audit Matters in the Independent Auditor's Report

Understanding ISA 701, "Communicating Key Audit Matters in the Independent Auditor's Report," as revised in November 2019 and updated in May 2022, is crucial for anyone preparing for the ICAEW ACA examination in Audit and Assurance. This standard plays a pivotal role in enhancing the transparency and usefulness of the auditor's report for stakeholders.

Overview of ISA 701
ISA 701 mandates auditors to report key audit matters (KAMs) in the independent auditor's report for audits of financial statements. KAMs are those matters that, in the auditor's professional judgment, were of most significance in the audit of the current period's financial statements. This requirement enhances the communicative value of the auditor's report and aids stakeholders in understanding those areas that required significant auditor attention.

Key Components of ISA 701
Identification of KAMs: Auditors identify KAMs based on areas of higher assessed risk of material misstatement, significant auditor judgments, or the effect of significant events or transactions on the audit.

Communication of KAMs: Each KAM must be described in the auditor's report, explaining why the matter was considered significant and how it was addressed in the audit.

Real-Life Application

Consider a company that underwent significant restructuring during the year. The auditor, in this case, might determine the accounting for this restructuring as a KAM due to its complexity and the significant judgment involved in evaluating its financial statement impact.

Impact of ISA 701 on Audit Quality

A study by the ACCA (Association of Chartered Certified Accountants) found that the introduction of KAMs has improved the quality of auditor reports by making them more tailored and informative. This change has led to a deeper engagement between auditors, management, and those charged with governance.

Examination Preparation Tips

Understand the Concept: Grasp the objective of KAMs - to enhance the communicative value of the auditor's report.

Real-Life Examples: Analyze real audit reports to see how KAMs are practically identified and communicated.

Case Studies: Review case studies or academic research papers that evaluate the impact of KAMs on audit practice.

Regulatory Updates: Stay updated on any changes or updates to ISA 701, as auditing standards are subject to change.

Practice Questions: Attempt practice questions that focus on identifying and communicating KAMs, as this will likely be a part of the examination.

Ethical Considerations: Understand the ethical implications in reporting KAMs, emphasizing auditor independence and objectivity.

705 (Revised June 2016) Modifications to the Opinion in the Independent Auditor's Report

Understanding ISA 705 (Revised June 2016) and its implications for the independent auditor's report is crucial for anyone studying for the ICAEW ACA qualification, particularly in the Audit and Assurance module. This standard addresses modifications to the auditor's opinion, which is a fundamental aspect of audit reporting.

What is ISA 705?
ISA 705, titled "Modifications to the Opinion in the Independent Auditor's Report," guides auditors on how to modify their opinion when they conclude that an unmodified opinion is not appropriate. It was revised in June 2016 to enhance clarity and effectiveness.

Types of Modifications
Qualified Opinion: This arises when the auditor concludes that misstatements are material but not pervasive to the financial statements. It's like saying, "Everything looks good, except for this specific part."

Adverse Opinion: Given when the auditor concludes that misstatements are both material and pervasive. This is a severe form of modification, essentially stating, "The financial statements are misleading."

Disclaimer of Opinion: Issued when the auditor cannot obtain sufficient appropriate audit evidence and concludes that the possible effects could be material and pervasive. It's akin to saying, "I can't be sure about the overall accuracy of these financial statements."

Key Considerations
Materiality and Pervasiveness: These are the two
critical dimensions. 'Materiality' refers to the
significance of an item's impact on financial statements.
'Pervasiveness,' on the other hand, refers to the extent to
which the misstatement affects the financial statements.

Audit Evidence: The lack of sufficient and appropriate
audit evidence can lead to a modification in the
auditor's opinion. This is often a complex area,
requiring auditors to exercise professional judgment.

Communication with Those Charged with Governance:
Auditors must discuss their findings and the type of
modification with the company's governance body (like
the board of directors) before issuing the report.

Real-Life Examples
Consider a company that has a significant portion of its
assets in a country with unstable economic conditions.
If the auditor cannot reliably assess the value of these
assets due to the economic instability, this may lead to a
disclaimer of opinion.

In another scenario, if a company has not properly
accounted for a material transaction, but the rest of the
financial statements are fine, the auditor might issue a
qualified opinion.

Impact on Stakeholders
The type of modification in an auditor's opinion
significantly impacts various stakeholders:

Investors and Creditors: They rely on auditors' opinions
to make informed decisions. A modification can

influence their perception of the company's financial health.

Management and Governance: A modified opinion can signal the need for better financial reporting practices and controls.

The Auditing Profession: Maintaining high standards in audit reporting enhances the profession's credibility.

706 (Revised June 2016) Emphasis of Matter Paragraphs and Other Matter Paragraphs in the Independent Auditor's Report

Understanding ISA 706 (Revised June 2016) regarding "Emphasis of Matter Paragraphs" and "Other Matter Paragraphs" in the Independent Auditor's Report is crucial for anyone preparing for the ICAEW ACA UK Audit and Assurance examination. Let's dive into this in a detailed and creative way, suitable for exam preparation.

1. Emphasis of Matter Paragraphs
Under ISA 706, an "Emphasis of Matter Paragraph" is used by auditors to draw attention to a matter presented or disclosed in the financial statements that is of such importance that it is fundamental to users' understanding of the financial statements. This doesn't mean the auditor disagrees with the presentation or disclosure.

Example: Suppose a company has faced a significant lawsuit that is prominently disclosed in the notes to the financial statements. An auditor might include an Emphasis of Matter Paragraph to ensure that readers do not overlook this potentially critical information.

2. Other Matter Paragraphs
Conversely, "Other Matter Paragraphs" are used to draw attention to any matter other than those presented or disclosed in the financial statements that is relevant to users' understanding of the audit, the auditor's responsibilities, or the auditor's report.

Example: An auditor might use an Other Matter
Paragraph to describe the reasons they cannot withdraw
from an audit after uncovering a significant matter
affecting the financial statements, which the
management refuses to rectify.

Real-Life Context
In practice, these paragraphs serve as a spotlight,
highlighting specific aspects of the financial reports or
audit process. For instance, after the financial crisis of
2008, auditors increasingly used Emphasis of Matter
Paragraphs to highlight significant uncertainties related
to going concern issues.

Technical Insight
Technically, the inclusion of these paragraphs does not
affect the auditor's opinion. They are not a substitute for
expressing a qualified or adverse opinion or for
disclosing a material uncertainty related to going
concern.

Recent Trends and Studies
Recent studies have indicated that the market reacts to
the inclusion of Emphasis of Matter Paragraphs,
particularly in cases where the emphasis is on going
concern or financial stability issues, suggesting that
these paragraphs play a crucial role in financial
reporting and market perception.

Exam Preparation Guide
For ICAEW ACA exams, understanding not just the
definitions but also the practical applications and
implications of these paragraphs is essential.
Candidates should practice identifying scenarios where
these paragraphs would be appropriate and how to
accurately draft them. Additionally, being aware of

recent trends and how these paragraphs affect stakeholder perception can be a key discussion point in exams.

710 Comparative Information – Corresponding Figures and Comparative Financial Statements

Understanding and addressing the topic of Comparative Information – Corresponding Figures and Comparative Financial Statements within the framework of ICAEW ACA UK Audit and Assurance is crucial for anyone preparing for the examination. This detailed guide aims to elucidate these concepts in simple English, infusing real-life examples and technical knowledge to facilitate comprehensive understanding.

Comparative Information – Corresponding Figures Concept: Comparative information in the form of corresponding figures is usually presented in financial statements. These figures are derived from the previous period and are displayed alongside the current period's figures for effective comparison.

Purpose: The primary purpose of presenting corresponding figures is to allow users of financial statements to perform a year-on-year comparison. This aids in identifying trends, assessing performance, and making informed decisions.

Auditor's Responsibility: An auditor's role includes ensuring that the corresponding figures are appropriately presented and are consistent with the current period's figures. They must also verify that these figures are free from material misstatement.

Real-Life Example: Consider a company that reported a significant increase in sales in the current year compared to the previous year. An auditor would scrutinize the corresponding figures to validate this increase and investigate any discrepancies.

Comparative Financial Statements
Definition: Comparative financial statements present complete sets of financial statements for two or more consecutive periods. Unlike corresponding figures, these statements offer a more comprehensive view of the financial position and performance over multiple periods.

Significance: They are particularly useful for long-term analysis, allowing stakeholders to observe trends and patterns over time. This can be crucial for strategic planning and forecasting.

Auditor's Evaluation: Auditors must evaluate whether the comparative financial statements adhere to the applicable financial reporting framework and are consistent in their presentation.

Practical Scenario: A business undergoing significant changes, such as mergers or acquisitions, would benefit from comparative financial statements. These statements would provide a clearer picture of the impact of such changes over different periods.

Key Differences and Similarities
Scope: Corresponding figures are a subset of comparative financial statements, focusing on specific line items.

Depth of Analysis: Comparative financial statements offer a deeper analysis as they include full sets of financial data.

Audit Approach: While the auditing approach is similar in terms of ensuring accuracy and compliance, comparative financial statements require a more extensive review process.

Real-Life Application

Imagine a retail company facing fluctuating sales. By examining corresponding figures, auditors can identify inconsistencies in sales reporting. In contrast, comparative financial statements might reveal broader financial trends, like a gradual increase in operating costs.

720 (Revised November 2019) (Updated May 2022) The Auditor's Responsibility Relating to Other Information

Understanding ISA 720 (Revised November 2019) (Updated May 2022), "The Auditor's Responsibility Relating to Other Information," is crucial for anyone preparing for the ICAEW ACA UK Audit and Assurance exams. This guidance is not only a technical requirement but also a real-world necessity for auditors.

Key Concepts of ISA 720:
Auditor's Responsibility: The auditor's main responsibility under ISA 720 is to read and consider the 'other information' in documents containing audited financial statements. 'Other information' may include directors' reports, management discussions, and analysis that accompany financial statements.

Identifying Inconsistencies: Auditors must identify material inconsistencies or misstatements of fact between the audited financial statements and other information. If an inconsistency is found, the auditor must take appropriate action, which could involve discussing it with management or amending the financial statements.

Assessment and Conclusions: The auditor is not required to audit the 'other information' but must read it to identify material inconsistencies with the audited financial statements or material misstatements of fact. If an uncorrected material misstatement is found, the auditor must report this in the auditor's report.

Real-Life Application:
Imagine an annual report of a company where the financial statements indicate a significant decline in revenue, but the director's report optimistically discusses increased market share. Here, the auditor must investigate this inconsistency, discuss it with management, and ensure the 'other information' does not provide a misleading impression of the financial statements.

Practical Considerations:
Communication with Management: Auditors should discuss their findings with management, especially when inconsistencies or misstatements are identified.

Understanding the Business: A deep understanding of the entity's business, including its environment and operations, is crucial for effectively applying ISA 720.

Documentation: Auditors must document their process of reading and considering other information, along with any identified inconsistencies or misstatements.

Recent Updates (May 2022):
The updates in May 2022 emphasize the importance of considering the wider context of 'other information' and ensuring it does not contradict the financial statements. This might involve more extensive discussions with management and possibly more robust documentation of the auditor's considerations.

800 (Revised) Special Considerations – Audits of Financial Statements prepared in Accordance with Special Purpose Frameworks

When preparing for the ICAEW ACA UK Audit and Assurance exam, understanding ISA 800 (Revised), "Special Considerations—Audits of Financial Statements Prepared in Accordance with Special Purpose Frameworks," is crucial. This standard provides guidance on how audits should be conducted when financial statements are prepared using a framework different from general-purpose frameworks like IFRS or GAAP.

Firstly, let's explore the nature of special purpose frameworks. These frameworks are used for preparing financial statements that are designed for specific needs of certain users. For instance, a company may prepare financial statements exclusively for regulatory purposes, or a trust might prepare financial statements solely for the benefit of its beneficiaries. The key here is that these frameworks are not designed for general use and therefore require special consideration in auditing.

Key Aspects of ISA 800 (Revised):

Objective of the Auditor: The primary objective remains to obtain reasonable assurance about whether the financial statements as a whole are free from material misstatement. However, the auditor must understand how the special purpose framework differs from general-purpose frameworks and how these differences impact the audit.

158

Compliance with Standards: Auditors must comply with all ISAs applicable to the audit unless stated otherwise in the ISA 800. This means even though the financial statements are prepared according to a different framework, the rigor and quality of the audit should not be compromised.

Audit Report Modifications: The auditor's report under a special purpose framework might look different. The auditor must clearly indicate the purpose for which the financial statements are prepared and state that the use of the financial statements may be limited to that purpose.

Understanding the Framework: A significant part of the auditor's responsibility is to understand the special purpose framework, how it is applied by the entity, and its adequacy for the intended users. This requires a deep dive into the specific requirements of the framework and how it aligns with the entity's purpose.

Real-Life Example: Consider a non-profit organization that prepares its financial statements solely for compliance with the requirements of a specific grant. The auditor must focus not only on the usual aspects of financial reporting but also on how these statements satisfy the grant's stipulations.

Materiality and Risk Assessment: The concepts of materiality and risk assessment may have different implications under a special purpose framework. Auditors need to tailor their approach to ensure that the material aspects of the financial statements according to the framework are adequately addressed.

Documentation: Auditors must thoroughly document their understanding of the special purpose framework, the entity's reason for using it, and how it affects the audit approach.

805 (Revised) Special Considerations – Audits of Single Financial Statements and Specific Elements, Accounts or Items of a Financial Statement

ISA 805 (Revised), titled "Special Considerations – Audits of Single Financial Statements and Specific Elements, Accounts, or Items of a Financial Statement", is an important topic for anyone preparing for the ICAEW ACA exams in Audit and Assurance in the UK. This guideline requires a specific focus, as it diverges from the general standards applicable to complete financial statements. Let's delve into this topic in a detailed yet simple manner, perfect for exam preparation.

Understanding ISA 805 (Revised)

At its core, ISA 805 deals with situations where an auditor is engaged to audit just a part of a financial statement – this could be a single financial statement (like a balance sheet) or specific elements, accounts, or items (like a schedule of sales). This is different from a typical audit, where the auditor assesses the entire set of financial statements.

Why ISA 805 is Important

The real-life importance of ISA 805 can be seen in various scenarios. For example, a company might need to provide a creditor with only an audited inventory list, or an investor may request an audit of revenue figures alone. In such cases, ISA 805 guides auditors on how to proceed while ensuring the integrity and quality of their work.

Key Aspects of ISA 805

Objective and Scope: The auditor must clearly understand and define the objective of the audit. This includes identifying the specific financial statement, element, account, or item to be audited.

Audit Planning and Performance: The planning phase under ISA 805 is crucial. The auditor needs to consider the unique aspects of the audit subject and plan accordingly. This might involve specialized procedures or a focus on particular risks.

Materiality and Risk Assessment: Unlike a full audit, the concept of materiality in ISA 805 is applied to the specific part being audited. The auditor must assess risks specific to the element in question.

Using Work of Others: If the audit relies on work done by others (e.g., experts in valuing a specific asset), the auditor needs to evaluate the adequacy of this work for their purposes.

Audit Report and Opinion: The audit report under ISA 805 should clearly describe the scope of the audit, including any limitations. The opinion given is also specifically on the part audited, not the entire financial statements.

Practical Example
Consider an auditor auditing a company's cash balances as per ISA 805. The auditor will specifically focus on cash-related controls, perform bank reconciliations, and maybe confirm balances with banks. This targeted approach differs from a full-scale audit where the focus is more comprehensive.

International Standards on Assurance Engagements (ISAEs) (UK)

3000 (July 2020) Assurance Engagements Other Than Audits Or Reviews Of Historical Financial Information

The ICAEW ACA (Institute of Chartered Accountants in England and Wales, Associate Chartered Accountant) in the UK places significant emphasis on Audit and Assurance as part of its curriculum. A key area within this is the understanding of Assurance Engagements Other Than Audits Or Reviews Of Historical Financial Information, as outlined in the ISAE (International Standards on Assurance Engagements) 3000, revised in July 2020.

Understanding the Scope of ISAE 3000 (Revised July 2020)

ISAE 3000 governs the assurance engagements that do not deal with audits or reviews of historical financial information. This typically includes engagements like assurance reports on internal controls, compliance with agreements, sustainability reports, and other non-financial information. The revised version from July 2020 brought in new considerations and updates, reflecting the evolving nature of the assurance landscape.

Key Elements of ISAE 3000

Objective and Scope: The standard defines a framework for conducting assurance engagements other than audits or reviews of historical financial data. It sets out the practitioner's responsibilities and provides guidance on the execution of such engagements.

Ethical Requirements: It emphasizes the importance of integrity, objectivity, and professional skepticism. A practitioner must adhere to these ethical principles to maintain the credibility of the assurance engagement.

Quality Control: It requires practitioners to implement quality control procedures that are consistent with the International Standard on Quality Control 1 (ISQC 1).

Performance Requirements: The standard mandates that practitioners plan and perform an assurance engagement with an attitude of professional skepticism, considering the possibility of material misstatement.

Evidence and Documentation: Practitioners must gather sufficient and appropriate evidence to reduce assurance engagement risk to an acceptably low level and must document this evidence systematically.

Real-World Applications

In practice, ISAE 3000 might be applied in several scenarios. For instance, a company might engage an auditor to provide assurance on its sustainability report. Here, the auditor will assess whether the report has been prepared in accordance with the applicable criteria (like GRI - Global Reporting Initiative standards) and express a conclusion.

Another example could be the assurance on internal control systems over financial reporting, where the auditor evaluates the effectiveness of these controls and provides a report.

Importance for ACA Exam Preparation

For ACA students, understanding ISAE 3000 is crucial. It's not just about memorizing the standard, but understanding its application in various contexts. Exam questions might include case studies where students have to apply their knowledge of ISAE 3000 in real-life scenarios. Hence, students should focus on:

Understanding the principles and concepts of ISAE 3000.
Recognizing the types of engagements covered under ISAE 3000.
Applying these concepts in case studies or hypothetical scenarios.
Staying Updated

Since standards like ISAE 3000 are subject to revision, it's important for students and practitioners to stay informed about the latest changes. This ensures their work remains compliant and relevant to current practices.

International Standards on Review Engagements (ISREs)

2400 (Revised) Engagements to Review Historical Financial Statements

The 2400 (Revised) Engagements to Review Historical Financial Statements is an essential area for any student or professional in the field of audit and assurance, particularly for those pursuing the ICAEW ACA qualification in the UK. Understanding this area requires diving into its key components, practical applications, and the nuances that make it a critical part of financial auditing.

1. Understanding the Scope and Purpose:
The 2400 (Revised) Engagements outlines the standards and practices for reviewing historical financial statements. Unlike an audit, which involves an in-depth examination, a review is intended to provide a limited level of assurance. It's like comparing a thorough health check-up (audit) to a general consultation (review). The goal is to ascertain whether anything material has come to the auditor's attention that suggests the financial statements are not in accordance with the applicable financial reporting framework.

2. Key Components:
Analytical Procedures: These are evaluations of financial information through analysis of plausible relationships among both financial and non-financial data. They often involve comparisons of recorded amounts to expectations developed by the auditor. Inquiries: This involves seeking information from knowledgeable persons inside or outside the entity. For

example, an auditor might inquire about the procedures for recording revenue.

Discussion with Management: This is crucial. Understanding management's perspective on the business and its financials can reveal insights not apparent in the financial statements alone.

3. Practical Application:

Imagine you are reviewing the financial statements of a small business. You notice that their inventory turnover rate has drastically changed from the previous year. Your analytical procedures might flag this as an area for further inquiry. Upon discussion with management, you might learn that they adopted a new inventory system that year.

4. Reporting:

The outcome of a review is a report that provides a conclusion on the financial statements. This conclusion is less comprehensive than an auditor's opinion but still holds significant value.

5. Real-World Implications:

In a study conducted by the Financial Reporting Council (FRC), it was noted that effective reviews can significantly enhance the quality of financial reporting. For example, a well-conducted review might catch misstatements that could have led to incorrect financial decisions.

6. Challenges and Considerations:

Professional Skepticism: An auditor must maintain a questioning mind and a critical assessment of audit evidence.

Understanding the Entity: It's vital to have a deep understanding of the business and its environment. For instance, if reviewing a tech company, awareness of tech industry trends is crucial.

7. Recent Developments:

The field of audit and assurance is continually evolving, with recent updates focusing more on the importance of technology and data analytics in the review process.

International Standards on Review Engagements (UK)

2410 (Revised May 2021) Review of Interim Financial Information Performed by the Independent Auditor of the Entity

The ICAEW ACA UK Audit and Assurance exam, particularly focusing on the revised May 2021 standard for the Review of Interim Financial Information Performed by the Independent Auditor of the Entity (ISRE 2410), encompasses a comprehensive range of topics crucial for aspiring auditors. This standard plays a pivotal role in ensuring the quality and reliability of interim financial reports.

Understanding ISRE 2410: ISRE 2410 guides auditors in reviewing interim financial information. It is essential for an auditor to understand that this review is less in scope than an audit but more than a mere compilation.

Real-Life Application: Consider a scenario where a publicly-traded company releases its half-year results. As an auditor under ISRE 2410, your role would be to review this information. This includes understanding the accounting practices used, assessing the materiality of financial statements, and evaluating whether they provide a true and fair view of the company's financial position.

Key Areas of Focus:

Materiality: You must understand the concept of materiality in the context of interim financial reporting.

What might be material in an annual report could be different in an interim report.

Analytical Procedures: These are essential in ISRE 2410. You'll compare the interim figures with annual financial statements, understand trends, and look for inconsistencies.

Inquiry and Discussion: Engage with management and others to gain a deeper understanding of the financial information, questioning and discussing any significant changes or unusual items.

Representation Letter: This is a key document where management confirms the validity of information provided to you. Ensure it is comprehensive and covers all aspects of the interim report.

Recent Changes and Their Implications: With the revision in May 2021, there's a heightened focus on the auditor's responsibility in relation to fraud, going concern, and subsequent events. This means you need to be more vigilant about these aspects during your review.

Case Studies and Research: Incorporating real-life examples and research findings into your study can enhance your understanding. For instance, research on common pitfalls in interim reporting can prepare you to be more attentive to these issues.

Examination Preparation: To excel in this part of the exam:

Familiarize yourself with the standard's text and practical guidance.
Practice with past exam questions and case studies.
Stay updated with any amendments or interpretative guidance issued by ICAEW or other regulatory bodies.

International Standards on Assurance Engagements (ISAEs)

3400 The Examination of Prospective Financial Information

The Examination of Prospective Financial Information, as covered in the ICAEW ACA UK Audit and Assurance curriculum, is a critical area for aspiring accountants and auditors. This examination revolves around understanding and evaluating financial forecasts and projections. It's essential to grasp this topic comprehensively, as it's a significant part of the professional accounting and auditing landscape.

1. Understanding Prospective Financial Information (PFI)

Prospective Financial Information refers to any financial information based on assumptions about events that may occur in the future and possible actions by the entity. It includes financial forecasts and projections. A financial forecast is an entity's expected financial position, results of operations, and cash flows, based on management's assumptions reflecting conditions it expects to exist and the course of action it expects to take. A projection is based on hypothetical assumptions about future events and management actions not necessarily expected to occur.

2. The Auditor's Role

Auditors are required to understand how management develops the PFI and the underlying assumptions. This involves evaluating the process used by management, the reasonableness of assumptions, the consistency of the PFI with historical patterns, and external economic or industry data. A real-life example is the auditing of a company's projected revenue growth in a new market. The auditor must assess whether the assumptions about market growth, competitive landscape, and the company's capabilities are reasonable and supported by evidence.

3. Assessing Assumptions and Methods

Auditors must critically assess the assumptions and methods used in preparing the PFI. For example, during the COVID-19 pandemic, many companies had to revise their financial forecasts considering the uncertain market conditions. Auditors had to scrutinize these revised forecasts, challenging assumptions about the duration of the pandemic and its impact on different sectors.

4. Evaluating the Presentation of PFI

The PFI should be presented in accordance with relevant financial reporting frameworks. The auditor evaluates whether the PFI is properly presented and all significant assumptions are adequately disclosed and clearly presented.

5. Reporting

The auditor concludes on the reasonableness of the PFI and reports to the stakeholders. This includes expressing an opinion on whether the PFI is prepared in accordance with the applicable framework and whether the underlying assumptions are reasonable.

6. Ethical Considerations

Ethical considerations in examining PFI include objectivity, professional skepticism, and confidentiality. Auditors must remain unbiased in evaluating management's assumptions and projections.

7. Real-World Application

An example can be drawn from the technology sector, where companies often project significant growth due to rapid innovation. Auditors have to balance optimism with realism, ensuring that the projections align with industry trends and technological advancements.

3402 Assurance Reports on Controls at a Service Organisation

Assurance Reports on Controls at a Service Organisation, commonly referred to as ISAE 3402 reports, are an integral part of the auditing and assurance landscape, especially within the framework of the ICAEW ACA (Institute of Chartered Accountants in England and Wales, Associate Chartered Accountant) qualification in the UK. These reports are designed to provide assurance over the controls at a service organization, which are relevant to user entities' internal control over financial reporting.

Understanding ISAE 3402 Reports
ISAE 3402 is an international assurance standard that prescribes Service Organisation Control (SOC) reports. The standard is primarily concerned with 'controls at a service organisation' which are relevant to user entities' (entities that use the services of the service organisation) internal control over financial reporting.

Types of ISAE 3402 Reports
Type I Report: Evaluates and reports on the design of controls at a service organization at a specific point in time.
Type II Report: Goes a step further by not only evaluating the design but also the operational effectiveness of these controls over a specified period.
Importance in the Audit Process
In an increasingly interconnected business environment, many companies outsource aspects of their business processes to service organisations. For example, a company might use a cloud service provider for data storage or a payroll processing company. ISAE 3402 reports provide assurance to the company's auditors

and stakeholders that the service organisation has adequate controls.

Real-Life Application
Consider a real-life scenario where a financial institution outsources its data processing to a third-party service provider. The financial institution's auditors, in conducting their annual audit, would rely on the ISAE 3402 report provided by the service provider to gain comfort over the data processing controls that impact the financial institution's financial reporting.

Preparing for ISAE 3402 in ACA Exams
When preparing for ACA exams, especially in the Audit and Assurance paper, it's crucial to understand the theoretical underpinnings of ISAE 3402. However, it's equally important to appreciate its practical application in real-world scenarios. Here are some tips:

Conceptual Understanding: Ensure you have a clear grasp of the objectives, scope, and types of ISAE 3402 reports.
Case Studies: Review real-life examples or case studies where ISAE 3402 reports have been pivotal. This will enhance your understanding of their application in different industry sectors.
Exam Questions: Practice past paper questions that involve scenarios requiring an understanding of ISAE 3402. This helps in applying theoretical knowledge to practical situations.
Updates in Standards: Keep abreast of any changes or updates to the ISAE 3402 standards, as the ACA exams often include recent developments in the field.
Professional Skepticism: Cultivate a mindset of professional skepticism, an essential skill in auditing, to

critically assess the effectiveness of controls reported in ISAE 3402 reports.

3410 Assurance Engagements on Greenhouse Gas Statements

Understanding and applying International Standard on Assurance Engagements (ISAE) 3410, "Assurance Engagements on Greenhouse Gas Statements," is crucial for auditors, especially in the context of the ICAEW ACA UK Audit and Assurance examination. ISAE 3410 provides a framework for assurance practitioners to evaluate an entity's greenhouse gas (GHG) statements. This is particularly relevant in today's world where environmental concerns and sustainability reporting are increasingly important.

Key Aspects of ISAE 3410:

Objective of the Engagement: The primary objective under ISAE 3410 is to express a conclusion on whether the GHG statement is prepared, in all material respects, in accordance with an applicable GHG framework. This involves assessing whether the reported GHG emissions reflect the organization's actual emissions.

Understanding the Entity and its Environment: It's essential to understand the entity's operations, internal controls, and GHG data management systems. For instance, if an entity is involved in heavy manufacturing, its GHG emissions will likely be significant, and the assurance engagement should be planned accordingly.

Assessment of Risks of Material Misstatement: This involves evaluating the risk that the GHG statement could be materially misstated. This could be due to errors, fraud, or non-compliance with the relevant GHG framework.

Evidence Gathering: The practitioner must gather sufficient and appropriate evidence to support their conclusion. This might involve physical inspections, data analysis, and reviewing the process of GHG data compilation.

Using the Work of Experts: Given the technical nature of GHG emissions, practitioners often rely on experts in environmental science or engineering to understand and evaluate the entity's emission calculations and reporting.

Reporting: The conclusion of the assurance engagement is reported in the assurance report. This report should clearly state the practitioner's opinion on the GHG statement.

Real-Life Application:

In a real-life scenario, consider an assurance engagement for a large automotive manufacturer. The auditor would need to understand the manufacturing processes, the sources of GHG emissions, and how these emissions are measured and reported. The auditor might consult with environmental experts to evaluate the accuracy of the GHG measurements and to understand any technical aspects related to emission reporting.

Technical Knowledge and Up-to-Date Information:

Auditors need to stay updated with the latest developments in environmental standards and reporting requirements. For instance, changes in environmental laws or advancements in GHG measurement technologies could impact the assurance engagement.

Exam Preparation Guide:

For the ICAEW ACA exam, candidates should focus on understanding the principles and procedures outlined in ISAE 3410. They should be prepared to apply these principles to hypothetical scenarios, similar to real-life situations. Practice questions might involve evaluating the adequacy of an entity's GHG reporting process or identifying risks in an assurance engagement on GHG statements.

Studying ISAE 3410 involves not just memorizing the standards but also understanding how to apply them in various contexts. Mock exams, real-life case studies, and staying informed about current environmental reporting trends are essential for effective exam preparation.

Other Guidance

Bulletin (August 2021): Illustrative Auditor's Reports on UK Private Sector Financial Statements

The ICAEW ACA UK Audit and Assurance Bulletin from August 2021 presents a critical resource for those pursuing the ACA qualification, particularly in the area of auditor's reports on UK private sector financial statements. This bulletin is integral for understanding the nuances and expectations in audit reports, crucial for anyone aiming to excel in their ACA exams and future professional practice.

Understanding the Bulletin's Key Points
Structure of Auditor's Reports: The bulletin emphasizes the standardized structure that auditor's reports must follow. This includes elements like the opinion, basis for opinion, key audit matters, and other reporting responsibilities. For instance, the 'Opinion' section is where the auditor expresses their view on the financial statements - whether they are a true and fair representation of the company's financial position.

Emphasis on Key Audit Matters (KAMs): KAMs are areas that, in the auditor's judgment, were of most significance in the audit. The bulletin guides on how to identify and report these matters effectively. For example, if a company has complex revenue recognition policies, this could be a KAM due to its significant judgment and estimation uncertainty.

Reporting on Other Information: Auditors are also responsible for reporting on other information included in the annual report. The bulletin guides on how to approach discrepancies or material misstatements found in this other information.

Going Concern: With the challenges posed by events like the COVID-19 pandemic, the bulletin underscores the importance of the going concern principle. Auditors must thoroughly evaluate and report on the company's ability to continue as a going concern.

Real-Life Application and Studies
Several studies and real-life examples underscore the importance of these elements. For instance, the collapse of Carillion highlighted failures in reporting key audit matters effectively. Research also shows that clear, concise auditor reporting increases stakeholder confidence in financial statements.

Examination Preparation Tips
Understand the Theory: Make sure you're clear on the theoretical aspects of audit reports. Understand each component and its purpose.

Analyze Case Studies: Look at real-life examples of audit reports. See how different auditors approach KAMs and other complex areas.

Practice Mock Reports: Writing mock reports based on hypothetical scenarios can be invaluable. It helps in understanding how to apply theory in practice.

Stay Updated: Regulations and expectations in audit and assurance are continually evolving. Keep up-to-date with the latest guidelines and bulletins like this one.

Critical Thinking: Develop your ability to analyze and critique audit reports. What could have been done differently? How could the report be more effective?

Milton Keynes UK
Ingram Content Group UK Ltd.
UKHW011950160224
437951UK00001B/139